Principles
in Practice

The Principles in Practice imprint offers teachers concrete illustrations of effective classroom practices based in NCTE research briefs and policy statements. Each book discusses the research on a specific topic, links the research to an NCTE brief or policy statement, and then demonstrates how those principles come alive in practice: by showcasing actual classroom practices that demonstrate the policies in action; by talking about research in practical, teacher-friendly language; and by offering teachers possibilities for rethinking their own practices in light of the ideas presented in the books. Books within the imprint are grouped in strands, each strand focused on a significant topic of interest.

Volumes in the Adolescent Literacy Strand

Adolescent Literacy at Risk? The Impact of Standards (2009) Rebecca Bowers Sipe

Adolescents and Digital Literacies: Learning Alongside Our Students (2010) Sara Kajder

Adolescent Literacy and the Teaching of Reading: Lessons for Teachers of Literature (2010) Deborah Appleman

Volumes in the Writing in Today's Classrooms Strand

Writing in the Dialogical Classroom: Students and Teachers Responding to the Texts of Their Lives (2011) Bob Fecho

Becoming Writers in the Elementary Classroom: Visions and Decisions (2011) Katie Van Sluys

Writing Instruction in the Culturally Relevant Classroom (2011) Maisha T. Winn and Latrise P. Johnson

Volumes in the Literacy Assessment Strand

Our Better Judgment: Teacher Leadership for Writing Assessment (2012) Chris W. Gallagher and Eric D. Turley

Beyond Standardized Truth: Improving Teaching and Learning through Inquiry-Based Reading Assessment (2012) Scott Filkins

Reading Assessment: Artful Teachers, Successful Students (2013) Diane Stephens, editor

Reading Assessment

Artful Teachers, Successful Students

Edited by

Diane Stephens
University of South Carolina

National Council of Teachers of English
1111 W. Kenyon Road, Urbana, Illinois 61801-1096

Staff Editor: Bonny Graham

Imprint Editor: Cathy Fleischer

Interior Design: Victoria Pohlmann

Cover Design: Pat Mayer

Cover Photo: Keith McGraw

NCTE Stock Number: 30773

Library of Congress Cataloging-in-Publication Data

Reading assessment : artful teachers, successful students / edited by Diane Stephens, University of South Carolina.
      pages cm
  Includes bibliographical references and index.
  ISBN 978-0-8141-3077-3 (pbk.)
  1. Reading. 2. Reading—Evaluation. I. Stephens, Diane, editor of compilation.
  LB1050.R3529 2013
  372.4—dc23
                                      2013013943

Contents

continued

Contents (continued)

Permission Acknowledgments

"To Beth's First Grade Teacher" reprinted by permission of Richard F. Abrahamson, University of Houston, *Houston Chronicle* 1984.

Figure 12 from *Talking, Drawing, Writing* by Martha Horn and Mary Ellen Giacobbe, copyright © 2007, reproduced with permission of Stenhouse Publishers. www.stenhouse.com

Excerpt from THE THREE QUESTIONS by Jon J. Muth. Copyright © 2002 by Jon J. Muth. Reprinted by permission of Scholastic Inc.

Figure 22 copyright 2005 by the National Council of Teachers of English. Reprinted with permission.

Introduction: The Art of Teaching

When I first started [the school year], I didn't know much about reading. Days and days and days I've been learning to be a strong reader. And now there is so much I can read. I am a thinking reader!

—Mathew,[1] age eight, at end of third grade

At the beginning of third grade, Mathew was reading more than a year below grade level and he did not like to read. By the end of the year, Mathew was not only reading at grade level, but he was also reading all of the books in Jeff Kinney's Diary of a Wimpy Kid series—for fun.

Mathew's teachers made this change possible. Mathew had a strong classroom teacher and strong supplemental small-group instruction from a reading interventionist. Both teachers had the support of a strong literacy coach. Mathew's three teachers, like all artful teachers, knew how to support and accelerate his progress as a reader. They had a broad and deep knowledge base—one founded on professional experience, deep reading, reflection, and conversations with others. They knew how children learn language, learn about language, and learn through language (Halliday, 1969, 1973, 1975, 1980); how to create learning communities (Peterson & Eads, 1990); and how to establish conditions for learning (Cambourne, 1987, 1995).

Mathew's teachers got to know their students and used this knowledge to inform instruction. To do this, they gathered data on a daily basis (including observations, interviews, and oral reading analyses) and systematically reflected on it (Whitin, Mills, & O'Keefe, 1991; Stephens, 1990; Stephens et al., 1996; Stephens & Story, 2000). Mathew's classroom teacher analyzed her data to determine the instructional focus for the whole class as well as for small groups and for individual students. For example, she learned that as a group, when her students came to an unknown word, they tended to substitute one that was visually similar even if it did not make sense in the passage, and so she taught whole-group lessons on the importance of predicting based on meaning and cross-checking using visual information. Similarly, she identified a subgroup of students who tended to skip words they did not know and keep on reading even though the text did not make sense. She placed these and other students in flexible small groups based on their instructional needs. She also noticed unique needs (e.g., the one student who loudly declared that he hated to read) and arranged her day so that she could spend one-on-one time with those students to better understand their needs and support them as readers.

Meanwhile, the interventionist used her data about Mathew and other students from his and other classrooms—all of whom were reading below grade level—to form small, pull-out groups based on instructional need. She then provided instruction customized to those needs. For example, the 9:00 group focused on making sense of reading (instead of sounding out every letter); the 9:30 group focused on problem-solving unfamiliar words; and the 10:00 group focused on understanding the text demands of various content area texts. Simultaneously, the literacy coach observed Mathew and other children in both the classroom and intervention settings and shared her observations with their teachers to ensure that instructional focus was consistent.

Mathew succeeded because all of his teachers—from the classroom teacher to the reading interventionist to the literacy coach—were committed to his success. Each saw herself as responsible for his progress as well as for that of every child in her care. Teachers who take such a stance continually strive to expand their knowledge base and to improve their ability to gather, make sense of, and use assessment data to inform instruction.

Responsibility versus Accountability

Teachers like Mathew's, who assume responsibility for every child as a reader, positively impact students' academic and life trajectories. When this happened in a local school district that I work closely with, elementary school children who began the year reading below grade level and had the support of a classroom teacher, a reading interventionist, and a literacy coach made two months of growth for every month they spent with the reading interventionist (see Table 1). Not all students are as fortunate. Consider the trajectory of most children who come to school and are soon identified as being "below grade level" in reading. Check in five years later and many of those children are still considered to be reading below grade level. This happens, in part, because most classroom teachers are not asked to take responsibility for these children. Instead, following federal guidelines, teachers refer them for testing; once tested—assuming at least an average IQ—the children are labeled as "learning disabled" (Ysseldyke, Thurlow, Mecklenburg, & Graden, 1984) and subsequently receive reading instruction from a special education teacher who, in most states, is not required to have advanced course work in reading. Under these conditions, it is no wonder that children make little progress as readers (Blachman, Schatschneider, Fletcher, & Clonan, 2003; Denton, Vaughn, & Fletcher, 2003; Hanushek, Kain, & Rivkin, 2002; Torgesen, Rashotte, Alexander, Alexander, & MacPhee, 2003).

In the late 1980s, when the now familiar standards movement was in its infancy, Dick Bodine, then an elementary school principal in a small town in Illinois, commented that he thought that *accountability* forced the gaze of educators outward, whereas *responsibility* focused the gaze inward (D. Bodine, personal communication, 1989). He thought that the new-at-the-time emphasis on accountability caused teachers to focus on what their principal wanted; principals, on what their superintendents wanted; and superintendents, on what their school board and other politicians wanted. In contrast, he argued that responsibility meant that teachers were focused on students, principals on students and teachers, and superintendents on students, teachers, and principals.

I have told dozens of people about the point Dick was making; I think it is even more important now than it was twenty years ago. Today, policymakers and stakeholders seem wedded to an accountability that overshadows responsibility. Consider, for example, local, state, and federal efforts to tie teacher pay to test scores of groups of children—as if it were not the daily responsibility for the growth of every child that matters but rather the accountability for the average score of subgroups of children on a standardized test given at the end of the year. This kind of misguided thinking leads to child-harming practices such as curricular narrowing (matching the content of instruction to only what is assessed); retaining students at one or more grade levels; and encouraging children to perform well on end-of-year testing while barely mentioning beginning-of-year tests—a move designed to deflate scores at the beginning of the year and inflate them at the end.

Table 1. Months of Growth per Month of Supplemental Support as Measured by Oral Reading Passages from *Dominie Reading and Writing Assessment Portfolio*[2]

Year	Total number of students	Months of growth per month of support
2007–2008	244	1.9
2008–2009	243	2.7
2009–2010	241	2.4
2010–2011	206	2.4

Note: The total number of students decreased because two schools decided to use computer programs instead of reading interventionists, and a third school chose to have the interventionist work alongside teachers in the classroom instead of providing supplemental instruction.

The Politics of Choosing Responsibility

In 2004, as part of the Individuals with Disabilities Education Act (IDEA), the federal government created a general education initiative known as Response to Intervention (RTI). RTI is a research-based alternative to the labeling of struggling readers as learning disabled. As part of RTI, districts can use up to 15 percent of their special education monies to ensure that all children receive the best possible reading instruction. This is a radical change in federal policy. Since the creation of the "learning disabled" label in 1963, large numbers of struggling readers have been placed in special education. The proportion of students receiving special education services for learning disabilities ranges from 10 to 20 percent and can be as high as 30 percent (Vellutino, Scanlon, & Tanzman, 1998). Nearly all of these students struggle as readers. In fact, Kavale and Reese (1991) estimate that 90 percent of the students identified as learning disabled before fifth grade read below grade level, while Nelson and Machek (2007) found that 79 percent of the students did so. Batsche, Curtis, Dorman, Castillo, and Porter (2007) determined that, in Florida, the figure was 95 percent.

However, research conducted over the last fifteen years shows that the number of students who struggle with reading and who truly have specific learning disabilities is relatively small. For example, Vellutino et al.'s early research into this topic (1998) suggested that perhaps only 1.5 to 3.0 percent of all struggling readers actually have learning disabilities. The authors argue that, instead of having learning disabilities, children struggle due to "inadequate pre-literacy experience, inadequate instruction or some combination of both" (p. 369). Since then, this theory has been supported by a number of studies demonstrating that, when provided with appropriate intervention by qualified personnel, most students make considerable progress as readers (McGill-Franzen, Allington, Yokoi, & Brooks, 1999; Scanlon, Vellutino, Small, Fanuele, & Sweeney, 2005; Torgesen, Alexander, Wagner, Rashotte, Voeller, & Conway, 2001; Vellutino et al., 1998).

By allotting monies to improve reading instruction, RTI has the potential to help the field shift from a focus on accountability to those outside the classroom to responsibility for the children in our classrooms. The initiative provides an opportunity for schools to determine how well students respond to appropriate instruction *before* they are referred for testing and subsequently labeled as in need of special education services. Under RTI, it becomes the responsibility of classroom teachers, not special education teachers, to "identify students' needs and help students succeed" (Wixson, Lipson, & Johnston, 2010, p. 6). Teachers who have an advanced understanding of the reading process are then able to provide supplemental instruction as needed. This supplemental instruction is often referred to as "Tier 2"; classroom instruction is considered "Tier 1."

Determining how to implement RTI so that all children receive the best possible instruction has led to difficult conversations in school districts across the country. School psychologists have traditionally used a discrepancy formula to determine whether a child should be labeled learning disabled. According to this formula, if the child has an average IQ score but reads below grade level, she or he is considered learning disabled. RTI challenges that assumption and, in so doing, creates tensions among school- and district-level stakeholders. Although the law calls on all classroom teachers to take responsibility for the reading progress of all of their students, many special education teachers and the psychologists who test and label children have long felt that the children who struggle are solely their responsibility.

Fortunately, Mathew's teachers are part of a strong literacy community within their district. There are coaches and interventionists at each of their elementary schools and strong support for literacy from the central office. Still, they—and many other teachers—are occasionally involved in politically loaded discussions with special education teachers and psychologists about what constitutes effective assessment, who should be responsible for it, and how assessment data can be used to inform instruction. The teachers' opinions—that, as responsible educators, they should continually assess their students, as well as their own teaching; that effective assessment is instructionally relevant; that it provides information that allows them to customize instruction for their whole class as well as for small groups and individual children—are not always shared by the special education teachers, school psychologists, and central office administrators.

To support their opinions, Mathew's teachers, like other teachers across the country, rely heavily on their own research, published research, and documents from their professional organizations. One particularly helpful source is *Standards for the Assessment of Reading and Writing* (SARW) (IRA–NCTE Joint Task Force on Assessment, 2010). Teachers who choose to take responsibility for their students can rely on the standards themselves and on the narratives contained in the introduction and following each standard. The introduction, for example, defines assessment as "the exploration of how the educational environment and the participants in the educational community support the process of students as they learn to become independent and collaborative thinkers and problem solvers" (p. 2). Statements like these help teachers frame conversations about the definition of assessment in their districts and lead them away from debates about particular tests toward a discussion of what data are necessary to ensure success for all students.

Teachers who choose responsibility know they have the backing of the International Reading Association (IRA) and the National Council of Teachers of English (NCTE) when they read in the SARW that the most useful assessments are "the formative assessments that occur in the daily activities of the classroom"

(p. 13) and that "teachers are the primary agents, not passive consumers, of assessment information. It is their ongoing, formative assessments that primarily influence students' learning" (p. 13). The SARW further reinforce the teachers' stance by stating that the field needs to "rely less on one-shot assessment practices and place more value on assessments of ongoing classroom performance" (p. 19).

When teachers are faced with arguments about the reliability or validity of teacher assessment versus standardized measures, they can again rely on the SARW. On reliability:

> [W]hen a teacher observes and documents a student's oral reading behaviors and uses that information to inform instruction, the data might not be as reliable, in a technical sense, as a norm-referenced test. However, in the context of a teacher's professional knowledge, they are more likely to have productive consequences. Often assessments are chosen for technical measurement properties rather than for the likelihood of productive consequences. . . . (p. 24)

On validity:

> [I]f any individual student's interests are not served by an assessment practice, regardless of whether it is intended for administration or decision making by an individual or by a group (as is the case with tests used to apply accountability pressure on teachers), then that practice is not valid for that student. (p. 12)

Finally, to support their argument that assessment should be instructionally relevant, teachers have ample support from the SARW:

> In the United States it is common to use testing for accountability, but the ultimate goal remains the improvement of teaching and learning. . . .
>
> If an educational assessment practice is to be considered valid, it must inform instruction and lead to improved teaching and learning. . . .
>
> The central function of assessment, therefore, is not to prove whether teaching or learning has taken place, but to improve the quality of teaching and learning and thereby increase the likelihood that all members of the society will achieve a full and critical literacy. . . . (pp. 15–16)

The introduction to the SARW and the short version of the standards themselves are reprinted on pages xvii–xxv of this book. Page numbers in cross-references, however, map to the published document, which is available online as a free download at https://secure.ncte.org/store/assessment-standards-revised.

Case Studies and Classroom Portraits by Teachers Who Chose Responsibility

It is not enough, of course, for teachers who choose responsibility merely to conduct and read research and to rely on documents like the SARW to help them put into practice meaningful assessment measures. They must also get to know their students. Such teachers take the time to really *see* each of the children in their classroom and to know each one deeply as a small and wonderful being. They come to know their students via assessment and then use their knowledge to customize instruction to help every child grow as a reader, writer, and learner—every day, every year. They are teachers who have found an artful way to marry assessment and instruction.

Artful teachers all across the country are making a difference. Twelve of them are featured here. Chapter 1 focuses on four reading interventionists who provide supplemental (Tier 2) instruction; they have written case studies about the first-through fifth-grade students with whom they work. Chapter 2 features eight Tier 1 classroom teachers who have collaborated with university faculty to write portraits of their preschool through fifth-grade classrooms. Reading across narratives, it is clear that all of these teachers have taken responsibility for the literacy progress of their students. In doing so, they live the assessment standards established by IRA and NCTE (2010).

The case studies presented here are all written by teachers from one school district. In many ways, they represent an ideal. When their district asked them to become reading interventionists, it simultaneously offered them three years of onsite graduate course work designed to help them excel at providing supplemental instruction. The district also arranged for them to be visited once a month by an individual from the district or the university who had reading expertise and who served as their coach. For three years, ten reading interventionists worked closely together to build their knowledge base. They read the literature, collected data on their students, and reflected deeply about the reading process and their role as reading interventionists. They explicitly named the beliefs they held about reading and used those beliefs to guide both assessment and instruction. The interventionists and their students also had what most teachers consider a luxury—small-group instruction, every day, for thirty to forty minutes, for as many weeks or months as was needed to help the students experience and be able to maintain success as readers.

The supplemental instruction they provided was and is needed because, while the research shows that most students can make about a year's progress for every year they are in school, it also suggests that approximately 17–18 percent of students need more support than can be provided by the classroom teacher (Vellutino et al., 1998). Under RTI, most often this support is provided to small groups of students in a setting outside of the classroom.

In Chapter 1, the case studies of the interventionists reveal the complexities and challenges of the children who, in the past, might have been considered learning disabled and sent to special education. These case studies are presented first because they provide a close look at the progress of children who struggle the most; they also make clear that reading interventionists do not have some "magic box" of special tricks—they simply supplement classroom instruction. The children's literacy futures are determined by the quality of the time they spend with their classroom teacher and with a reading interventionist. By taking a close look at each of the four children foregrounded in the case studies, classroom teachers who are reading this book will be able to make connections and see with new eyes the children in their own classrooms whom they worry about most.

In the classroom portraits in Chapter 2, classroom teachers and the university professors with whom they collaborated make explicit how classroom teachers have managed to do the same kind of "looking closely and listening carefully" (Mills, O'Keefe, & Jennings, 2004) as the interventionists were able to do in the case studies. They discuss their assessment tools, including talking, watching, and recording, and describe how they make sense of the data they collect and use it to inform instruction.

Following each of the case studies and classroom portraits is a list of the assessment tools and instructional moves used by that teacher. It is the deep hope of all of us as authors that these case studies and classroom portraits prove useful to other teachers who choose to take responsibility for the progress of every child in their classrooms.

Notes

1. Except for Louise Ward in Portrait 3, all teachers' names are authentic. Except for Cameron in Portrait 5, all student names are pseudonyms.

2. The *Dominie Reading and Writing Assessment Portfolio* (DeFord, 2004) is a multifaceted reading, writing, and spelling assessment system. It allows the teacher to gather information on phonemic awareness, phonics (onset and rimes), letter knowledge, core reading and writing words, phoneme representation and spelling, story writing/composition, concepts about print and sources of information (narrative and informational texts), and oral and silent reading (accuracy, fluency, pace, self-correction, and comprehension). The oral and silent reading assessment consists of a series of paperback booklets, ranging from ten to twenty-three pages, and leveled from kindergarten through eighth-grade reading levels. The booklets are both fiction and nonfiction, and the topics, text characteristics, and genres are tied to grade-level expectations.

Standards for the Assessment of Reading and Writing, Revised Edition

A publication of the IRA–NCTE Joint Task Force on Assessment

Introduction

This document provides a set of standards to guide decisions about assessing the teaching and learning of literacy. In the past 30 years, research has produced revolutionary changes in our understanding of language, learning, and the complex literacy demands of our rapidly changing society. The standards proposed in this document are intended to reflect these advances in our understanding.

Readers of this document most likely share common experiences with respect to literacy and assessment. For example, in our own school days, we were directed to read to get the correct meaning of a text so that we could answer questions put to us by someone who already knew that correct meaning or by a test (often multiple choice) for which the correct answers were already determined. In order to develop assessment practices that serve students in an increasingly complex society, we must outgrow the limitations of our own schooling histories and understand language, literacy, and assessment in more complex ways. Literacy involves not just reading and writing, but a wide range of related language activities. It is both more social and more personal than a mere set of skills.

The need to understand language is particularly important. Language is not only the object of assessment but also part of the process of assessment. Consequently, any discussion of literacy assessment must include a discussion of language—what it is, how it is learned, and how it relates to assessment. Before we state our assessment standards, then, we will give an overview of what we mean by assessment and how we understand language and its relationship to assessment.

The Nature of Assessment

For many years, a transmission view of knowledge, curriculum, and assessment dominated and appeared to satisfy our social, political, and economic needs. Knowledge was regarded as a static entity that was "out there" somewhere, so the key educational question was, How do you get it from out there into students' heads? The corollary assessment question was, What counts as evidence that the knowledge really is in their heads? In a transmission view, it made sense to develop educational standards that specified the content of instruction before developing assessment procedures and engagements.

In the 1920s, notions of the basic purposes of schooling began to shift from an emphasis on the transmission of knowledge to the more complex nurturing of independent and collaborative learning and of problem solving. This shift has gained increasing prominence in today's postindustrial society, with its ever-expanding need for workers with strong communication skills and dispositions toward problem solving and collaborating. A curriculum committed to independent learning is built on the premise that inquiry, rather than mere transmission of knowledge, is the basis of teaching and learning.

Standards for the Assessment of Reading and Writing

This shift from knowledge transmission to inquiry as a primary goal of schools has important implications for assessment. In a knowledge-transmission framework, tests of static knowledge can suffice as assessment instruments. Students are the participants who are primarily accountable (either they have the knowledge or they don't), with teachers held accountable next. Policymakers, including school board members, trustees, or regents, are the primary recipients of assessment data. An inquiry framework changes the role of assessment and the roles of the participants. Within this framework, assessment is the exploration of how the educational environment and the participants in the educational community support the process of students as they learn to become independent and collaborative thinkers and problem solvers. This exploration includes an examination of the environment for teaching and learning, the processes and products of learning, and the degree to which all participants—students, teachers, administrators, parents, and board members—meet their obligation to support inquiry. Such assessments examine not only learning over time but also the contexts of learning.

Inquiry emphasizes different processes and types of knowledge than does knowledge transmission. For example, it values the ability to recognize problems and to generate multiple and diverse perspectives in trying to solve them. An inquiry stance asserts that while knowledge and language are likely to change over time, the need for learners at all levels (students, teachers, parents, administrators, and policymakers) who can solve new problems, generate new knowledge, and invent new language practices will remain constant. An inquiry perspective promotes problem posing and problem solving as goals for all participants in the educational community. For example, inquiry values the question of how information from different sources can be used to solve a particular problem. It values explorations of how teachers can promote critical thinking for all students. And it raises the question of why our society privileges the knowledge and cultural heritage of some groups over others within current school settings.

Inquiry fits the needs of a multicultural society in which it is essential to value and find strength in cultural diversity. It also honors the commitment to raising questions and generating multiple solutions. Various stakeholders and cultural groups provide different answers and new perspectives on problems. Respecting difference among learners enriches the curriculum and reduces the likelihood of problematic curricular narrowing.

Just as the principle of inquiry values difference, so the principle of difference values conversation over recitation as the primary mode of discourse. In a recitation, it is assumed that one person, the teacher, possesses the answers and that the others, the students, interact with the teacher and one another in an attempt to uncover the teacher's knowledge. In a conversation, all of the stakeholders in the educational environment (students, parents, teachers, specialists, administrators, and policymakers) have a voice at the table as curriculum, standards, and assessments are negotiated. Neither inquiry nor learning is viewed as the exclusive domain of students and teachers; both are primary concerns for all members of the school community. For example, administrators ask themselves hard questions about whether the structures they have established support staff development, teacher reflection, and student learning. School board members ask themselves whether they have lived up to

Standards for the Assessment of Reading and Writing

the standards they have set for themselves and their schools to provide teachers and students with the resources they need to guarantee learning opportunities.

Quality assessment, then, hinges on the process of setting up conditions so that the classroom, the school, and the community become centers of inquiry where students, teachers, and other members of the school community investigate their own learning, both individually and collaboratively. The onus of assessment does not fall disproportionately upon students and teachers (which is often the case in schools today); instead, all those inquiring into the nature and effectiveness of educational practices are responsible for investigating the roles they have played. Different members of the school community have different but interacting interests, roles, and responsibilities, and assessment is the medium that allows all to explore what they have learned and whether they have met their responsibilities to the school community.

The Nature of Language

Language is very much like a living organism. It cannot be put together from parts like a machine, and it is constantly changing. Like a living organism, it exists only in interaction with others, in a social interdependence. Language is a system of signs through and within which we represent and make sense of the world and of ourselves. Language does not contain meaning; rather, meaning is constructed in the social relationships within which language is used. Individuals make sense of language within their social relationships, their personal histories, and their collective memory. In order to make sense of even a single word, people take into account the situation and their relationship with the speaker or writer.

Take, for example, *family*, a word often used as if all members of society agree on its meaning. The word may mean different things in different contexts, however, whether cultural, situational, or personal. To a middle-aged white person whose parents moved across country with their two children and who repeated that experience herself, *family* may mean the nuclear family structure in which she grew up and in which she is raising her own children. To someone from a different culture—perhaps an African American or Asian American—the word may conjure images of the constellation of grandparents, aunts, uncles, and cousins who live together or near one another. So, meaning may vary from one person to another, as in this case, where meanings attached to the word *family* are likely to differ depending on one's own experience in the family or families one has lived with. Thus, individuals make different sense of apparently similar language to the extent that their cultural and personal histories do not coincide. Consequently, when we attempt to standardize a test (by making it the same for everyone), we make the tenuous assumption that students will all make the same meaning from the language of our instructions and the language of the individual items.

Different cultures also have different ways of representing the world, themselves, and their intentions with language. For example, in any given cultural group, people have different ways of greeting one another, depending on the situation (e.g., a business meeting, a funeral, a date) and on their relationship to each other. Our own language practices come from our cultural experience, but they are also part of the collective practice that forms the

Standards for the Assessment of Reading and Writing

culture. Indeed, the different ways people use language to make sense of the world and of their lives are the major distinguishing features of different cultural groups.

At the same time, language is always changing as we use it. Words acquire different meanings, and new language structures and uses appear as people stretch and pull the language to make new meanings. Consequently, the meaning that individuals make from language varies across time, social situation, personal perspective, and cultural group.

The Nature of Literacy

The nature of literacy is also continually changing. Today, many children read more online than offline. They are growing into a digital world in which relatively little reading and writing involves paper, most reading and writing involves images as much as print, and writing (both formal and less formal, the latter including e-mail, texts, Facebook posts, etc.) is becoming equal to, or even supplanting, reading as a primary literacy engagement. The tools of literacy are changing rapidly as new forms of Internet communication technology (ICT) are created, including (at the time of writing) bulletin boards, Web editors, blogs, virtual worlds, and social networking sites such as Ning and MySpace. The social practices of literacy also change as a result of using digital technologies, as does the development of language. New literate practices are learned and refined just by existing from day to day in what has become known as the mediasphere. For example, living with cell phones leads to texting, which changes how people view writing and how they write, and frequenting Web 2.0 sites, such as the video-sharing service YouTube, privileges a visual mode and shapes both attention to and facility with other modes of meaning making. The literacies children encounter by the end of their schooling were unimagined when they began.

Reading and writing online changes what it means to read, write, and comprehend. Literacy practices now involve both the creation and use of multimodal texts (broadly defined). Creating multimodal texts requires knowing the properties and limitations of different digital tools so that decisions can be made about how best to serve one's intentions. Participating in social networking sites, for example, requires new literacy practices; new literacy practices shape how users are perceived and how they construct identities. This leads to new areas needing to be assessed, including how youths create and enhance multiple identities using digital tools and virtual spaces. We now need to be concerned with teaching and assessing how students take an idea in print and represent it with video clips for other audiences. Similarly, we must be concerned about the stances and practices involved in taking an idea presented in one modality (e.g., print) and transcribing or transmediating it into another (e.g., digital video), and we must consider what possibilities and limitations a particular mode offers and how that relates to its desirability over other modes for particular purposes and situations. Children use different comprehension strategies online and offline, and assessments of the two show different pictures of their literacy development. Online readers, by choosing hypertext and intertext links, actually construct the texts that they read as well as the meanings they make. New multimodal texts require new critical media literacies, linked to classical critical literacy notions of how media culture is created, appropriated, and subsequently colonizes the broader notions of culture—for example, how youth culture is defined by and used to define what youths do, what they buy, and with whom they associate.

Standards for the Assessment of Reading and Writing

The definitions of literacy that have dominated schooling and are insisted on by most current testing systems are inadequate for a new, highly networked information age. Failure to help all students acquire literacies for this age will not serve them or society well. Not to teach the necessary skills, strategies, dispositions, and social practices is to deny children full access to economic, social, and political participation in the new global society. Not to assess these capabilities will result in curricular neglect and a lack of information to inform instruction.

The Learning of Language

By the time children arrive at school, they have learned to speak at least one language and have mastered most of the language structures they will ever use. Through social interaction, using the language they hear around them from birth, they have developed, without their awareness, the underlying rules of grammar and the vocabulary that give meaning to the world as they see it. Nonetheless, we often teach language in schools as if children came to our classrooms with little or no language competence. Nothing could be further from the truth. Children can request, demand, explain, recount, persuade, and express opinions. They bring to school the ability to narrate their own life histories. They are authors creating meaning with language long before they arrive at school.

As children acquire language in social interaction, particularly with others whose language is different or more complex, they gain flexibility in using language for different purposes and in different social situations. Learning a second language or dialect roughly parallels learning the first, for learning any language also entails becoming competent in the social relationships that underlie it. Children also develop fluent use of language without explicit knowledge of or instruction in rules and grammars. This means that grammars and rules are taught most productively as tools for analyzing language after it has been acquired. Even adults who have considerable facility with the language frequently can articulate few, if any, grammar or language rules. In spite of this truism, we often go about assessment and instruction in schools as if this were not the case.

Furthermore, although we pretend otherwise, language is not acquired in any simple hierarchical sequence.

In some ways, school actually plays a modest role in language acquisition, the bulk of which occurs outside of school. In schools, we must learn to teach language in a way that preserves and respects individuality at the same time that we empower students to learn how to be responsible and responsive members of learning communities. In other words, we must respect their right to their own interpretations of language, including the texts they read and hear, but we must help them learn that meaning is negotiated with other members of the learning communities within which they live and work. To participate in that negotiation, they must understand and be able to master the language practices and means of negotiation of the cultures within which they live. They must understand the language conventions that are sanctioned in different social situations and the consequences of adhering to or violating those conventions.

Although much of our language is learned outside school, studying language is the foundation of all schooling, not just of the language arts. For example, in science class, we make knowledge of the world using language. To study science, then, we must study the language through which we make scientific knowledge, language that has an important impact on the curriculum. If in reading and writing about science the language is dispassionate and distancing, then that is part of the knowledge that students construct about science, part of the way they relate to the world through science.

The Assessment of Language

Our description of language and language learning has important implications for the assessment of language, first because it is the object of assessment (the thing being assessed) and second because it is the medium of assessment (the means through and within which we assess). Instructional outcomes in the language arts and assessment policies and practices should reflect what we know about language and its acquisition. For example, to base a test on the assumption that there is a single correct way to write a persuasive essay is a dubious practice. Persuading someone to buy a house is not the same as persuading someone to go on a date. Persuading someone in a less powerful position is not the same as persuading someone in a more powerful position—which is to say that persuasive practices differ across situations, purposes, and cultural groups. Similarly, that texts can (and should) be read from different perspectives must be taken as a certainty—a goal of schooling not to be disrupted by assessment practices that pretend otherwise. To assert through a multiple-choice test that a piece of text has only one meaning is unacceptable, given what we know of language.

Moreover, to the extent that assessment practices legitimize only the meanings and language practices of particular cultural groups, these practices are acts of cultural oppression. When our assessments give greater status to one kind of writing over another—for example, expository writing over narrative writing—we are making very powerful controlling statements about the legitimacy of particular ways of representing the world. These statements tend to be reflected in classroom practices.

When we attempt to document students' language development, we are partly involved in producing that development. For example, if we decide that certain skills are "basic" and some are "higher level," and that the former need to be acquired before the latter, that decision affects the way we organize classrooms, plan our teaching, group students, and discuss reading and writing with them. The way we teach literacy, the way we sequence lessons, the way we group students, even the way we physically arrange the classroom all have an impact on their learning.

The Language of Assessment

Because it involves language, assessment is an interpretive process. Just as we construct meanings for texts that we read and write, so do we construct "readings" or interpretations of our students based upon the many "texts" they provide for us. These assessment texts come in the form of the pieces that students write, their responses to literature, the various assignments and projects they complete, the contributions they make to discussions, their behavior in different settings, the questions they ask in the classroom or in conferences, their performances or demonstrations involving language use, and tests of their language competence. Two different people assessing a student's reading or writing, his or her literate development, may use different words to describe it.

Standards for the Assessment of Reading and Writing

In classrooms, teachers assess students' writing and reading and make evaluative comments about writers whose work is read. The language of this classroom assessment becomes the language of the literate classroom community and thus becomes the language through which students evaluate their own reading and writing. If the language of classroom assessment implies that there are several interpretations of any particular text, students will come to gain confidence as they assess their own interpretations and will value diversity in the classroom. If, on the other hand, the language of classroom assessment implies that reading and writing can be reduced to a simple continuum of quality, students will assess their own literacy only in terms of their place on that continuum relative to other students, without reflecting productively on their own reading and writing practices.

When teachers write report cards, they are faced with difficult language decisions. They must find words to represent a student's literate development in all its complexity, often within severe time, space, and format constraints. They must also accomplish this within the diverse relationships and cultural backgrounds among the parents, students, and administrators who might read the reports. Some teachers are faced with reducing extensive and complex knowledge about each student's development to a single word or letter. This situation confronts them with very difficult ethical dilemmas. Indeed, the greater the knowledge the teacher has of the student's literacy, the more difficult this task becomes.

But it is not just classroom assessment that is interpretive. The public "reads" students, teachers, and schools from the data that are provided. Parents make sense of a test score or a report card grade or comment based on their own schooling history, beliefs, and values. A test score may look "scientific" and "objective," but it too must be interpreted, which is always a subjective and value-laden process.

The terms with which people discuss students' literacy development have also changed over time. For example, in recent history, students considered to be having difficulty becoming literate have acquired different labels, such as *basic writer, remedial reader, disadvantaged, learning disabled, underachiever, struggling student,* or *retarded reader.* These different terms can have quite different consequences. Students described as "learning disabled" are often treated and taught quite differently from students who are similarly literate but described as "remedial readers."

Further, assessment itself is the object of much discussion, and the language of that discussion is also important. For example, teachers' observations are often described as informal and subjective and contrasted with test results that are considered "formal" and "objective." The knowledge constructed in a discussion that uses these terms would be quite different from that constructed in a discussion in which teachers' observations were described as "direct documentation" and test results as "indirect estimation."

Assessment terms change as different groups appropriate them for different purposes and as situations change. Recent discussions about assessment have changed some of the ways in which previously reasonably predictable words are used, belying the simplicity of the glossary we include at the end of this document. For example, the term *norm-referenced* once meant that assessment data on one student, typically test data, were interpreted in comparison with the data on other students who were considered similar. A norm-referenced

Standards for the Assessment of Reading and Writing

interpretation of a student's writing might assert that it is "as good as that of 20 percent of the students that age in the country." Similarly, the term *criterion-referenced assessment* once meant simply that a student's performance was interpreted with respect to a particular level of performance—either it met the criterion or it did not. Recently, however, it has become much less clear how these terms are being used. The line between criterion and norm has broken down. For example, *criterion* has recently come to mean "dimension" or "valued characteristic." *Norm* has come to be used in much the same sense. But even in the earlier (and still more common) meaning, most criteria for criterion-referenced tests are arrived at by finding out how a group of students performs on the test and then setting criteria in accord with what seems a reasonable point for a student's passing or failing the test.

In other words, assessment is never merely a technical process. Assessment is always representational and interpretive because it involves representing children's development. Assessment practices shape the ways we see children, how they see themselves, and how they engage in future learning. Assessment is social and, because of its consequences, political. As with other such socially consequential practices, it is necessary to have standards against which practitioners can judge the responsibility of their practices.

Using This Document

In what follows, each standard is presented as a statement with a brief explanatory paragraph. The standard is then expanded with additional detail. The text concludes with case studies that illustrate the standards' implications in both large-scale and classroom assessments.

The central premise of the standards is that quality assessment is a process of inquiry. It requires gathering information and setting conditions so that the classroom, the school, and the community become centers of inquiry where students, teachers, and other members of the school community examine, individually and collaboratively, their learning and ways to improve their practice.

The Standards

1. The interests of the student are paramount in assessment.
2. The teacher is the most important agent of assessment.
3. The primary purpose of assessment is to improve teaching and learning.
4. Assessment must reflect and allow for critical inquiry into curriculum and instruction.
5. Assessment must recognize and reflect the intellectually and socially complex nature of reading and writing and the important roles of school, home, and society in literacy development.
6. Assessment must be fair and equitable.
7. The consequences of an assessment procedure are the first and most important consideration in establishing the validity of the assessment.

Standards for the Assessment of Reading and Writing

8. The assessment process should involve multiple perspectives and sources of data.

9. Assessment must be based in the local school learning community, including active and essential participation of family and community members.

10. All stakeholders in the educational community—students, families, teachers, administrators, policymakers, and the public—must have an equal voice in the development, interpretation, and reporting of assessment information.

11. Families must be involved as active, essential participants in the assessment process.

For the complete Standards *document, see http://www.ncte.org/standards/assessmentstandards/ introduction or https://secure.ncte.org/store/assessment-standards-revised.*

Case Studies from Artful Reading Interventionists

From 2007 to 2010, I worked closely with a group of ten reading interventionists[1] from School District Five of Lexington and Richland County in South Carolina and with Robin Cox, who, in 2007, was the coordinator for English language arts in that district. The reading interventionists were responsible for providing supplemental instruction to students who were reading below grade level. In a Response to Intervention (RTI) model, the interventionists were considered Tier 2.

Over a three-year period, the interventionists took graduate-level reading courses from me every summer and during the last year. For the first and second year, they took their courses during the year from adjunct faculty. For all three years, Robin, I, and, as applicable, the adjunct who taught their courses visited with the interventionists monthly to observe them working with children and to debrief with them afterward. The fourth year we met monthly to discuss the literature on RTI. Those years were a kaleidoscope of experiences—reading, thinking, teaching, observing, reflecting—and out of those experiences we co-constructed a list of our beliefs about what students needed to know and be able to do in order to progress as readers. We entitled that list "A Theory of What Matters for Readers" (WM; see Figure 1).

Figure 1. A theory of what matters for readers.

We believe that it matters that students:
1. Understand that reading is meaningful
2. Believe in their ability to make sense of texts
3. Consider reading a pleasurable event
4. Spontaneously self-monitor
5. Have knowledge, skills, and strategies to problem-solve to ensure meaning
6. Use this information flexibly
7. Use this information independently
8. Use this information with increasingly sophisticated texts

We have come to believe that children need to have in place a three-part theory of themselves as readers: they need to understand that reading is a meaning-making process (WM 1), believe in their ability to make sense of print (WM 2), and find pleasure in reading (WM 3). When all three are in place, the child has what we consider a *generative* theory of reading. Children who have such a theory almost always spontaneously self-monitor—they stop when the text does not make sense (WM 4). When that happens, children need a repertoire of skills and strategies to problem-solve flexibly, independently, and with increasingly complex text (WM 5–8).

We were able to construct the "What Matters" list because we read the professional literature carefully and deeply and paid close attention to the readers with whom we worked. We noticed what they were doing, considered multiple possibilities, developed hypotheses, tested out those hypotheses, and made more observations. We continued this cycle until we had a theory about each child as a reader and then used it to plan instruction. This reflective framework is called the hypothesis–test process (Omalza, Aihara, & Stephens, 1997; Stephens, 1990; Stephens et al., 1996; Stephens & Story, 2000).

We also developed and tested a theory about how to best support the needs we identified. We concluded that our first responsibility was to help each child develop a generative theory of learning. We realized that if a child did not yet understand that reading was a meaning-making process (WM 1), we needed to help the child develop that understanding before she or he could progress as a reader. Similarly, if a child understood meaning-making but did not believe in his or her ability to make sense of text (WM 2), then we had to help the child shift that belief. If the first two aspects of the child's theory were in place, we needed to determine whether the child found reading pleasurable enough to choose to read (WM 3).

If the child held all three beliefs, the child held a generative theory of reading and almost always self-monitored (WM 4). As appropriate, we could then begin to help the child develop and/or expand the skills and strategies she or he needed to problem-solve text (WM 5–8). This insight feels like common sense to us now, but in the beginning, we too often tried to teach problem-solving skills and strategies (e.g., "read ahead and come back to that part"; WM 5) to children who had not yet developed generative theories (WM 1–3) and were not self-monitoring (WM 4). We were trying to teach skills and strategies that children could not yet use.

As part of getting to know a child as a reader, we tried to find the conditions under which the child could be successful. For example, perhaps we noticed that when a particular child read a text in which she or he knew 92 percent of the words and came to a word she or he did not know, the child substituted a visually similar nonsense word and kept reading. If, in response, we varied genre and text demands and/or topics, we might find that the same child, when reading a predictable text written two years below grade level, accurately figured out unknown words or substituted a word that made sense. If we switched one or more of those factors, we found that the child abandoned meaning and reverted to skipping words. Once we understood the conditions under which the child problem-solved words and maintained meaning, we knew where to begin instruction. Sometimes, of course, there were no conditions under which this occurred spontaneously; when this happened, we had to create those conditions.

To help a child develop a theory of reading as meaning-making (WM 1), for example, those conditions could include reading to or with the child, having authentic conversations with him or her about a book, providing opportunities for the child to have meaningful conversations about a book with others, and/or making sure the child has extensive blocks of time during the day to read appropriate books of choice. Having the child spend an extended amount of time experiencing reading as meaningful increases the odds that she or he will come to understand and hold onto the meaningfulness of text when it becomes more complex.

For a long time, we thought of "appropriate" texts as "just right" texts. Over time, however, we started referring to appropriate books as "fun and easy." We made this shift because when children talked about just right books, they seemed to associate them with the "work" of reading. We wanted reading not to be thought of as work but as something one did for pleasure. Referring to books as fun and easy helped us to help the children view books differently. To determine the "fun" part, we looked for signs in the child of interest and engagement. To determine the "easy" part, we looked for books in which children would know 98–99 percent of the words. When the books met these criteria, we increased the odds that we could simultaneously help the child focus on meaning (WM 1), build self-confidence (WM 2), and find reading pleasurable (WM 3).

This does not mean that we ignored skills and strategies (WM 5–8). To the contrary, we helped children learn about them. However, we did not do this so the child could master a particular skill or strategy, but so the mastery of those skills or strategies would enable the child to develop one or more aspects of his or her personal theory—that reading is a meaning-making process (WM 1), that he or she can make sense of text (WM 2), and that reading is pleasurable (WM 3). For example, in the first case study presented here, Kathy Vickio helps David develop his sight vocabulary and word attack skills, not as an end in itself but to help him build his confidence as a reader—to help reading feel "easy" to him. We have had considerable success with this approach, as we explained in Table 1. On average, children seen by the reading interventionists made two months of text-level growth, as assessed by the *Dominie* (DeFord, 2004), for every month of support they received.

Most of the children who have received intervention services in this district either did not yet approach reading as a meaning-making process or did not believe in their ability to make sense of text (see Table 2 for 2009–2010 and 2010–2011 patterns). In the case studies that follow, interventionists focus on children with these two most dominant needs. Kathy Vickio tells the story of David, a repeating first grader who did not believe in his ability to make sense of text. In the second case, Lee Riser explains the progress of Rosalee, a third grader whose family spoke Spanish at home and who focused more on getting words "right" than on the meaning of the text. Next, Anne Downs details her experiences with Joseph, a fourth grader who had made little progress in the past and considered reading a meaningless chore he had to endure. And finally, Beth Sawyer focuses on Faith, a fifth grader who, like first grader David, did not believe in her ability to make sense of text. Across all four case studies, the "What Matters" framework informs both assessment and instruction.

Table 2. Instructional Needs of Children Seen in Intervention, 2009–2010 and 2010–2011

Instructional needs of children seen in intervention

A. Year: 2009–2010 / Total number of students: 241

	Instructional focus	Percentage of K–5 students seen in intervention with that need
1	Understands reading is a meaning-making process	41%
2	Believes in ability to make sense of print	20%
3	Finds reading pleasurable	12%
4	Spontaneously self-monitors	15%
5	Has a variety of skills and strategies for problem-solving	4%
6	Uses those skills and strategies flexibly	3%
7	Uses those skills and strategies independently	3%
8	Uses those skills and strategies across increasingly complex text	3%

B. Year: 2010–2011 / Total number of students: 206

	Instructional focus	Percentage of K–5 students seen in intervention with that need
1	Understands reading is a meaning-making process	28%
2	Believes in ability to make sense of print	14%
3	Finds reading pleasurable	14%
4	Spontaneously self-monitors	20%
5	Has a variety of skills and strategies for problem-solving	13%
6	Uses those skills and strategies flexibly	7%
7	Uses those skills and strategies independently	3%
8	Uses those skills and strategies across increasingly complex text	1%

Case Study 1: David, Repeating First Grader

Reading Interventionist Kathy Vickio

Instructional Focus: Does not yet believe in ability to make sense of text (WM 2)

David was a European American repeating first grader who was new to the school. In the one-on-one intervention setting, he was a delightful, pleasant child. In the classroom, he was often argumentative; he always wanted everything he did to be "right."

On the first-grade *Dominie* (DeFord, 2004) "Core Reading Words" list, David knew one word. His text level was a 1B, which equates to the middle of kindergarten. When he "read" a book, he virtually ignored the print and told a story using pictures. He was reluctant to look at the words on the page. When asked to do so, he became nervous and most often refused. When he did attempt to read a word, he silently moved his lips, trying to sound it out, but often he was not successful and easily became frustrated. When I asked him why he did not want to try a word he had whispered (and which was correct), he looked at me and said,

"I don't think it is right." I felt that David was often unwilling to use the skills and strategies he did possess because to do so would be to risk being "wrong."

I hypothesized that David had given up on himself and that he did not feel he could be successful as a reader. He preferred telling stories using pictures because he was good at it and it was safer. I realized that this meant I would need to be extremely careful with the books that David read. They needed to have highly predictable stories and vocabulary. In addition, the language I used with David during instruction would have to be thoughtful, positive, and supportive. If he felt he was struggling with a piece of text, he would react negatively.

I began using texts with David that I knew would be easy for him and that contained words I knew he could get "right." I encouraged him to talk a lot about the story before he began to read and told him explicitly about some of the words he could expect to see in the book. So that David could feel successful as a reader, he and I read a lot of easy books when he was with me; his classroom teacher also greatly increased David's time with easier books.

Slowly, David began to take more risks as a reader. Even so, when I used the *Dominie* (DeFord, 2004) leveled texts to document his progress, if he struggled with a single word, he immediately became frustrated and shut down. When I asked David how he felt when I used the *Dominie* texts, he first stated that they did not bother him. However, when I started reading the book introduction from inside the front cover (e.g., "This is a story about Tom and his dad. . . ."), he immediately exclaimed, "That's it. When you talk like that it makes me nervous." I realized that I needed to modify my language during assessments so that David would feel more confident. From that point on, whenever it was time to document his growth using a *Dominie* text, I reviewed the book introductions before David entered the room. Then I simply talked to him about the book. This seemed to help David relax and to use with the *Dominie* texts the skills and strategies he already possessed and was learning from his teachers.

I also began asking David to write high-frequency words so that he would feel more confident with them. Each day I wrote a few sight words on a dry erase board and David would try to find them in books he had read. I also had him "make and break" other words from his books using magnetic letters. These tasks were easy for David. He loved doing them and they became his favorite activity when he came for reading. Although he did not immediately transfer his increased sight vocabulary to his reading, this word work helped increase his confidence—it helped him develop a generative theory.

By March, when I analyzed his miscues, David was using both visual and meaning cues when he read. At the end of May (the ninth month of first grade), David successfully managed a Level 7 *Dominie* (DeFord, 2004), which equates to a reading level of the ninth month of first grade. He had received twenty weeks (five months) of supplemental support and was showing fifteen months of growth. On the *Dominie*, David was reading at grade level but was a year behind relative to age level. He had 97 percent accuracy and 100 percent comprehension. He was at the 65th percentile on his Measures of Academic Progress (MAP) test (Northwest Evaluation Association, 2008). David no longer panicked or became frustrated when he had to stop to look closely at a word to figure it out. He was excited about reading, asked to take books home, and loved to talk about the stories he read.

I supported David over the summer and plan to work with him at the beginning of the next year. Now that he is consistently taking risks and problem-solving words, I want to help him continue to build his skills and strategies so he can use them flexibly and independently with increasingly complex texts. His success as a reader has helped reduce his frustrations in the classroom. I expect David to have a very successful second-grade year.

See Figure 2 for a list of the assessment tools and instructional methods I used to help David.

Figure 2. What Kathy did to help David believe in himself as a reader (WM 2).

Assessment Tools

Observation

Listening

Inquiry (asking questions to understand)

Dominie "Core Reading Words" list

Dominie "Oral Reading Passages"

Modified miscue analysis

Measures of Academic Progress (MAP)

Systematic reflection on data using hypothesis–test process

Instructional Moves

Used easy texts.

Talked about story before reading.

Introduced words that might be new.

Wrote high-frequency words.

Made and broke words.

Modified *Dominie* procedures.

Ensured that all teacher comments help develop agency.

Provided ample time for reading.

Case Study 2: Rosalee, Third Grader

Reading Interventionist Lee Riser

Instructional Focus: Does not yet understand that reading is about making meaning (WM 1)

Rosalee was a third-grade, Latina female in her first year of reading intervention. She was new to our school and had attended another elementary school in our district for kindergarten through second grade. Rosalee had a sister in fifth grade and another older sister in her twenties who had recently moved out of the house with her baby and into her own apartment. Rosalee's mother spoke Spanish and there was no other adult in the household. Therefore, Rosalee spoke predominantly Spanish at home. She was fluent in English, though she did not yet have a good handle on academic vocabulary.

At the beginning of the year, Rosalee was reading at the 2.2 grade instructional level as measured by the *Dominie* (DeFord, 2004). I used a modified form of miscue analysis (original by Goodman & Burke, 1972; modified by Stephens, 2005) to determine that, when Rosalee came to words she did not know, she used meaning 33 percent of the time and some visual information 67 percent of the time. Because Rosalee was using meaning less than half the time and visual more than half the time (and not necessarily to figure out the same unknown word), her use of this information was inefficient and ineffective. Rosalee said that when she came to a word she didn't know, she "split the word up." She looked at the end of the word first, then at the beginning of the word, and put it all together. I asked her what she would do if that didn't work, and she said she would ask someone for help. It seemed that Rosalee was confused about how to problem-solve words visually. After reflecting on these data and talking with Rosalee, I was pretty sure that she thought reading was about getting words right.

My first task was to make sure that Rosalee understood that reading is supposed to make sense. I put her in a small group with two other students who I felt shared her theory of reading, and I helped them select books they were interested in reading. They first read Alyssa Satin Capucilli's Biscuit series and, over the course of the next month, we established a Fancy Nancy book club based on Jane O'Connor's series. Rosalee and her group subsequently read all the books in the series. Because the series was easy for them, when they came to a word they did not know, such as *glorious* or *extraordinary*, they thought about what would make sense and were able to figure out the word or come up with a synonym.

Rosalee was also an active participant in selecting fun and easy library books each week. She discovered Mo Willems's Pigeon series, such as *Don't Let the Pigeon Drive the Bus* (2003). Rosalee soon got the other girls involved in reading the Mo Willems books and then went a step further by initiating an impromptu readers theater. The girls took turns being one of the two characters or the narrator.

Although my instructional focus was on meaning-making, Rosalee was simultaneously coming to believe in her ability to make sense of text and finding reading pleasurable. Once this generative theory was firmly in place, I used a variation of Kathleen Visovatti's (1994) bookmark strategy (see also Johnson, 2006) to make a paper hand with strategies on each finger that Rosalee could use to problem-solve unfamiliar words (see Figure 3).

Rosalee was reading at home almost every night because she really enjoyed doing so. She had discovered a new series—Kate DiCamillo's Mercy Watson mysteries. As she read more, Rosalee's use of meaning cues increased dramatically to 75 percent and her self-correction ratio became 1:2. By the end of the school year, Rosalee was reading at the 3.5 grade level, with 98 percent accuracy and 100 percent comprehension. She was learning to use a variety of problem-solving strategies flexibly and independently. Rosalee selected a variety of different book genres from our classroom library to read over the summer and obtained a public library

Figure 3. Rosalee's strategy hand.

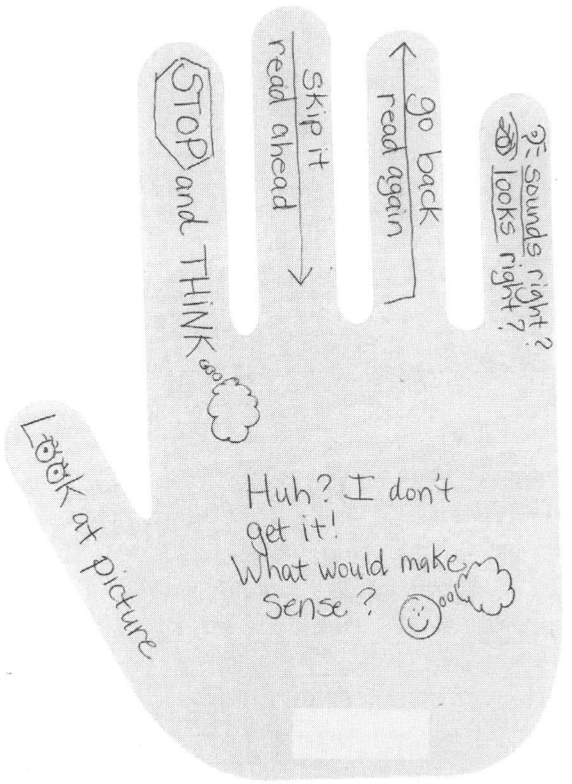

card. She planned to check books out weekly. Rosalee was teaching her mother how to speak English and had begun to show her how to read with bilingual books from the school library. As Rosalee explained, "I am showing my mom how to read English with very easy books so she understands."

See Figure 4 for a list of assessment tools and instructional methods I used to help Rosalee.

Figure 4. What Lee did to help Rosalee understand that reading is a meaning-making process (WM 1).

Assessment Tools

Observation

Listening

Inquiry (asking questions to understand)

Dominie "Oral Reading Passages"

Modified miscue analysis

Systematic reflection on data using hypothesis–test process

Instructional Moves

Used easy texts.

Provided time for reading.

Provided time for talk about books.

Provided access to a range of books in the intervention setting.

Allowed students to choose high-interest books.

Encouraged synonym substitution.

Taught problem-solving strategies.

Encouraged reading at home.

Encouraged personal library card.

Provided books to take home.

Case Study 3: Joseph, Fourth Grader

Reading Interventionist Anne Downs

Instructional Focus: Did not yet understand that reading was about making meaning (WM 1)

Joseph was a fourth grader who originally came to Reading Intervention with three other boys, all African American. Most of the time, the students I see are quite at ease and eager to participate, but Joseph would not sit with the group. Instead, he sat away from us with his arms crossed; if asked to join the group, he would start crying and shake his head vigorously. For the first three weeks, Joseph continued to act upset, resistant, and disengaged. He was suspended within the first month of school for exhibiting violent behavior.

Joseph had been retained in the first grade, and much of his prior instructional history was focused on phonics and fluency. He started second grade reading on a 1.3 grade level and finished that year reading on a 1.5 grade level. In third grade, his reading progressed another two months, finishing the year at a 1.7 grade level. At the beginning of fourth grade, Joseph was reading with 96 percent accuracy a passage written at a second-grade level. He read large portions within a text without comprehending but understood enough of the words to answer the comprehension questions. To figure out an unknown word, Joseph used meaning 35 percent of the time and full or partial visual information 78 percent of the time

(75–80 percent is ideal for both). On the *Dominie* (DeFord, 2004), Joseph scored in the first stanine for both phonemes and spelling. He had not been labeled learning disabled because there was not a considerable discrepancy between projected reading level and his current reading level (which was two years below grade level). In our district, such children are referred to as "DNQ" (does not qualify for special education). Before coming to see me, however, Joseph had spent two years with a special education teacher in a small reading group.

I decided to work with Joseph one on one. In that setting, he was less upset and his body language was much more approachable. Slowly he became willing to talk with me about the books I read aloud to him. At first I did most of the oral thinking and reacting. Within two weeks, with prompting, Joseph started sharing thoughts and reactions two or three times per text. However, he had not yet offered thoughts or reactions independently. I decided to ask Charles, a boy from Joseph's classroom, to join us. I had noticed in several school settings (i.e., regular classroom, lunch, recess) that Joseph and Charles had become friendly, and I thought that Joseph might share his thoughts and reactions more readily with Charles present. Charles was lower in accuracy and fluency than Joseph, but both boys lacked the understanding that reading is meaningful. I wanted to see if Joseph would feel confident enough to engage Charles in a meaningful conversation about books since he was, in some ways, a more sophisticated reader than Charles. Under these conditions, Joseph did in fact begin to engage with and react to text as we read independently. He was becoming a much more active and invested reader.

At the beginning of the calendar year, however, Joseph continued to view reading as something he had to "go through" in order to stay out of trouble with teachers. He also still thought that the point of reading was to get words right by sounding them out. This was particularly detrimental to him because using sound–symbol information was not one of his strengths.

To help Joseph shift from his theory that reading was about getting words right to a theory of reading as meaning-making, I asked him to tell me about a time he felt happy and successful reading a book. He said, "Once I read a Jimmy Neutron Christmas book [Beechen, 2003] and it was good. I liked that book." Knowing that to help Joseph shift his theory I had to find text that he really cared about, I located several Jimmy Neutron books online. Joseph had substantial background knowledge about the books, as he had seen all of the episodes on TV. This helped him read the books with ease and enjoyment. We laughed a lot. He shared his knowledge with me so I could understand the books as well as he did. He helped me gain understanding, and once we named that together, Joseph was a different reader and person in the intervention setting. The focus on meaning—and his confidence—led him to actively, joyfully, and consistently make meaning with these texts.

We spent four weeks reading all of the Jimmy Neutron books. During that time, I was able to show Joseph how to use meaning to solve words; I then released that responsibility to him and he took it on independently. Together, we named every skill and strategy he used. I modeled how to stop, think, and react during reading. Before turning a page, Joseph always made sure he understood all that he had read. He also understood and could talk about the tools that helped him read independently.

When we finished the Jimmy Neutron books and were discussing what we would read next, Joseph asked if he could read chapter books. I felt a strong need to honor his desire to fit in with the kid culture, but I was not willing to risk a move backward—to Joseph's previous, visual theory of reading—by introducing books that were too difficult for him. He had only truly been making meaning for four weeks. I did, however, feel that it would be beneficial for Joseph to become interested in a series; I thought that building a foundational understanding of character, setting, and structure/format would serve him well as an independent reader. Seeking guidance, I went to his classroom during independent reading to see what the other children were reading. Diary of a Wimpy Kid books were the prevalent choice, but I did not think they would help Joseph learn to make meaning independently. The Diary of a Wimpy Kid books contain the random thoughts of a middle school boy; the narrative is disjointed and the structure is unusual. Before Joseph read something like this, I thought he should first experience success with text that has a common structure and connected, cohesive thoughts. For Joseph at this point, *Diary of a Wimpy Kid* would have been better as a book on CD that he could "read along" with.

Two boys whom Joseph admired were reading Mary Pope Osborne's Magic Tree House books; his teachers also read these books aloud to him and I knew that he enjoyed them. I researched the books and found that the first one in the series, *Dinosaurs before Dark* (Osborne, 1992), was leveled 2.5. I read the book and believed that Joseph could manage the text with help. The book did not represent Joseph culturally, nor did he have a personal interest in dinosaurs, but it was the first book in the series and contained a lot of necessary information about the series. When I mentioned the book to him, he was so happy that I decided to go forward. I read the first three chapters of *Dinosaurs before Dark* to Joseph as he read along. As I read, I asked, "If you had been reading alone, are there any parts that might not have been easy to read?" Joseph showed me two places where he thought it might not have been easy reading for him—both were names of dinosaurs; he did not possess enough background knowledge or oral vocabulary to have known them. We took notes on the characters that Joseph brilliantly named "Keep It Straight Notes" (see Figure 5).

We thought together and reacted together. I had preread the fourth chapter and explained to Joseph the meaning of one word, *mutant*, that I was worried would discourage him. With this information, a strong foundational understanding of the characters and settings, and an exciting, suspenseful feeling about these two children possibly being eaten by dinosaurs, Joseph read the fourth chapter as I read along and did a modified miscue analysis (original by Goodman & Burke, 1972; modified by Stephens, 2005). He read the chapter with high accuracy and limited expression but talked about what he was thinking as he did so. From then on, we shared reading responsibility. I preread the chapters so that I could read the

---

Figure 5. Joseph's "Keep It Straight Notes."

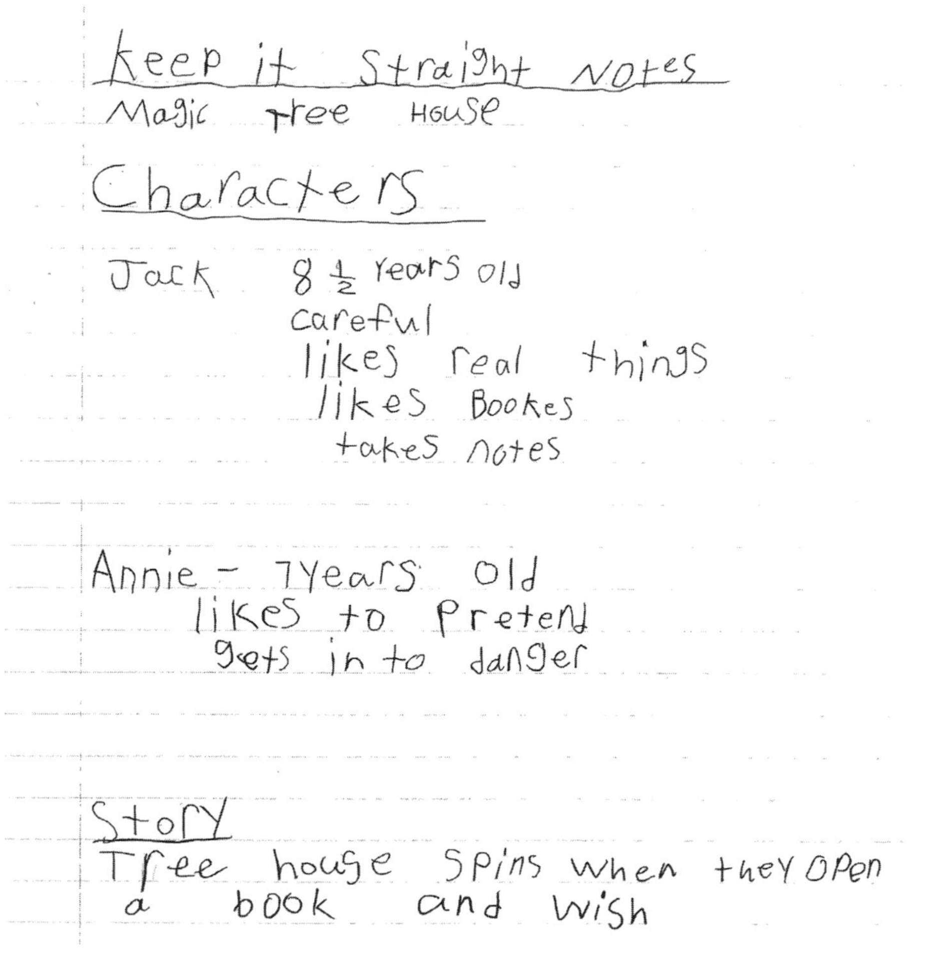

---

more challenging chapters as he read along. He read the less challenging chapters while I read along and did a modified miscue analysis. As we read this book, Joseph solidified his ability to solve unknown words flexibly and maintained a deep understanding of the text as he read. He had successfully read a chapter book. When we finished, his eyes were shining and he was smiling.

At Joseph's request, we progressed to another Magic Tree House book. Because he had shared with me his interest in civil rights, I selected *Civil War on Sunday* (Osborne, 2000a), which was leveled at 2.3. I read the first three chapters aloud and Joseph read along, making "Keep It Straight Notes" without assistance.

With this strong comprehension foundation, Joseph was able to read the rest of the book to me. During this time, we talked about and I modeled how expression and intonation help us better understand a story. Joseph's expression and intonation gradually began to match the text; he built the feeling of suspense with his reading and reactions. I modeled how to reread text to clarify when meaning broke down. Joseph began rereading text to clarify if he did not fully understand it on the first read.

Joseph was intrigued by the historical aspect of these stories and went on to read a level 2.2 book, *Revolutionary War on Wednesday* (Osborne, 2000b), independently and with high accuracy and thorough comprehension. He internalized, thought about, and reacted to everything he read. Joseph did not articulate a shift in his belief in himself at this point (that is not really who he is—he guards those deep thoughts), but his whole being had changed by the end of this book. He was more relaxed and definitely a happy, smiling reader.

From this point forward, Joseph came to me at all times of the day, asking for books he could read. On his own, he checked out graphic novels from the library that were about the Revolutionary War and the Civil War. Joseph held the key to his becoming a reader. He held it. He shared it with me. I listened. I really listened. Everything he said to me was of great importance. While we moved on to several other meaningful reading experiences, the important shift in Joseph's theory of reading happened in the experiences previously described. Joseph taught me to be careful not only to listen with a *miscue ear* (a colloquial term likely invented by Goodman, Watson, and Burke, based on their work with miscue analysis: Goodman & Burke, 1972; Goodman, Watson, & Burke, 1987), but also to listen closely to who readers are as people. Joseph's path was Jimmy Neutron and fitting in with kid culture. I just guided him along.

By the end of the year, Joseph understood that reading is a meaning-making process. He was more confident as a reader and more engaged in reading. He was enjoying books that he was interested in and that were relevant to him. He understood that efficient readers think and react while they read—not just at the end of the text. When Joseph came to a word he did not know, 70 percent of the time he used meaning and coupled that with visual information to achieve comprehension. I considered this a "balanced" use of cue systems. Joseph's score on the *Dominie* "Sentence Writing and Spelling" assessment (DeFord, 2004) was in the fourth stanine; there were still many words he had not encountered in print. His Text Reading Level on the *Dominie* "Oral Reading Passages" assessment (DeFord, 2004) grew from an equated level of 1.9 to 2.9. While this may seem like "only" one year's growth in one year, it is more than four times the progress he made in either of the two previous years (two months' growth in second grade and another two months in third).

I will continue to support Joseph's literacy learning next year. Now that he understands that reading is making meaning, believes in his ability to make sense of text, and finds reading pleasurable, I will focus on helping him problem-solve informational and content area reading. Because of the limited time Joseph had with texts prior to fourth grade, there are still many grade-level words that he has not encountered. With extensive independent reading and continued support from me, I believe he will make more than one year's growth next year.

See Figure 6 for a list of assessment tools and instructional methods I used to help Joseph.

Figure 6. What Anne did to help Joseph understand that reading is a meaning-making process (WM 1).

Assessment Tools

Observation

Listening

Inquiry (asking questions to understand)

Dominie "Oral Reading Passages"

Modified miscue analysis

Systematic reflection on data using hypothesis–test process

Instructional Moves

Read aloud.

Thought aloud.

Talked about books.

Found a partner/friend.

Chose high-interest books.

Scaffolded to make books manageable.

Honored background knowledge.

Taught problem-solving strategies.

Modeled stop–think–react.

Named observed strategies.

Taught note-taking.

Introduced new vocabulary.

Demonstrated expression/intonation.

Case Study 4: Faith, Fifth Grader

Reading Interventionist Beth Sawyer

> Instructional Foci: (a) Did not yet believe in her ability to make sense of text (WM 2); (b) needed to stay focused on reading as meaning-making as text demands increased (WM 1)

Faith was a European American fifth grader who had transferred to our school district during her fourth-grade year. She entered our school before end-of-year testing, and based on her MAP test results (Northwest Evaluation Association, 2008) and recommendations from her classroom teacher, the school assessment team recommended her for reading intervention.

When I began providing reading intervention services to Faith in the fifth grade, I gave her the *Dominie* (DeFord, 2004) Text Level 10. This text equates to a 3.5 grade level. She was successful on this assessment in all three areas: comprehension (88 percent), accuracy (96 percent), and fluency (3 out of 4 on the *Dominie* rubric). She had twelve miscues and six self-corrections. All of her miscues were meaningful and they were all very similar visually to the words in the text. The only comprehension question Faith missed was related to vocabulary used in the story.

In my initial conversations with Faith, her comments suggested that she did not see herself as a "good" reader. She stated that she only liked books that she was interested in and that had short words. Books that were thick and had longer words were too difficult. Faith also believed that good readers know all the words, and that she knew such readers. She felt that if she read more, she would be a better reader and smarter, yet she was unwilling to read any more than she had to. Faith's teacher had informed me that Faith was not completing homework reading assignments. When I asked her why she was not reading what she needed to for class, Faith said she could not read the books and would not pass fifth grade anyway. During the first few weeks of intervention, it appeared that Faith did not want to engage with text or with me. She often said that she was bored or not feeling well. She would put her head down or ask to use the restroom or to go the health room. She would sit with folded arms and a slouchy posture in her chair. It was difficult at times to get her to look at the page of text, much less read it. One day another teacher entered the classroom during the time that I was with Faith. Faith immediately told the teacher that the reason she was with me was that she could not read.

During this time, I was providing Faith with opportunities to read appropriately leveled text about animals, a topic in which she had expressed an interest. As she read aloud, I pointed out all of the things she was doing well in meeting the demands of the text and holding onto meaning as she read. This became part of our daily routine. I took notes about Faith's reading and about my conversations with her. I reflected on these notes, trying to figure out under what conditions she could be successful so that I could teach to her needs using her strengths (see Figure 7). I concluded that Faith understood that reading was a meaning-making process but did not have the belief that she could make sense of text. She needed a boost in confidence that reading was something she could do.

Based on these conclusions, I decided to let Faith become more involved in choosing books that she wanted to read rather than books chosen by me or her classroom teacher. She needed to read books that she felt comfortable in reading and that she felt she could manage independently. She chose picture books, including those written by P. D. Eastman (e.g., *Are You My Mother?*). I was uncomfortable at first with her choices because they were below her instructional level. However, Faith enjoyed reading these books and would laugh and share parts she found humorous. She would also point out things she noticed and inferred about the story or the characters. Our conversations about text became less about what I wanted her to notice about text and more about what Faith wanted to share about her reading. She seemed more at ease with me and more willing to take risks in her reading and to share her now positive thoughts about reading. Then, while

Figure 7. Anecdotal notes about Faith.

	Hypothesis – Test Sheet		
Name: FAITH	Grade: 5TH Date: 11/11		Page: 9 of __
Teacher: SAWYER	Observer: _____		
Observations	**Interpretations**	**Hypotheses**	**Curricular Decisions**
(F) STATES THAT READING IS BORING BUT SOMETIMES FUN. ALSO, SHORT WORDS MEANS IT'S EASY TO READ, LONG WORDS MAKE IT HARD. IF SHE READS ABOUT PUPPIES AND KITTENS w/ SHORT WORDS THAT WOULD NOT BE BORING	- to (F) BORING IS DIFFICULT - IF IT'S TOO BORING, ITS EASY. - EASY IS HIGH INTEREST - (F) ONLY INTERESTED IN READING ABOUT WHAT SHE LIKES - DIFFICULT IS LONG WORDS, EASY IS SHORT WORDS	looking OVER THE LAST 3 OBSERVATIONS THE QUESTION FORMS - UNDER WHAT CONDITIONS WILL (F) STAY ENGAGED WITH TEXT OR DISENGAGE	OBSERVE (F) READING APPROPRIATE LEVEL TEXT: - WHAT STRATEGIES DOES SHE HAVE IN PLACE? - WILL SHE STOP WHEN IT DOESN'T MAKE SENSE OR DOES SHE DO ANYTHING AT ALL WHEN MEANING IS LOST?

Stephens, 1990

she continued to enjoy picture books, she also began to express an interest in short chapter books.

Faith's demeanor had also changed. Her attitude and outlook were very different from the fifth grader who entered my room at the beginning of the year. She smiled more readily, was more compliant when asked to read, and no longer said she was bored or not feeling well. She seemed to enjoy reading and was engaged in text. I remember watching her one day when she was in the classroom rocking chair in a relaxed position, with all of her attention focused on her reading. If I had had a camera, I would have taken a picture.

Now that her confidence seemed to be increasing, I decided to focus on Faith's skills and strategies. She seemed to believe that "good readers" got "all the words right," which made her reluctant to make meaningful predictions or semantically acceptable substitutions. I needed to help her rely more on meaning when she encountered unknown words. To do this, I continued to provide Faith with books that she found interesting—ones that she *wanted* to read—and I also made sure that these books were easy for her to read (no higher than a 3.5 grade level). When she came across a word she did not know, I encouraged her to use what she already knew about the text to determine that word or another one that was consistent with the meaning of the text. Once she was consistently doing this with me, I encouraged Faith to continue doing this when she was reading independently. I observed her during those times, and she and I chatted about her use of this strategy. As she took on this strategy, she stopped trying to get all the words right and shifted her focus to understanding the text.

By the end of the year, Faith was able to independently manage a *Dominie* (DeFord, 2004) Level 11B, which equates to a 4.3 reading level. Her accuracy was 99 percent; she received 4 out of 4 for fluency, and her comprehension was 75 percent. She missed items that referred to concepts she did not understand and that were not clearly explained in the text, such as *maiden voyage* and *second-class tickets*. During the four months I worked with her, Faith made seven months' growth on the *Dominie*. She was reading more difficult text with higher accuracy while maintaining the meaning of the text. She used meaning to predict unfamiliar words and then cross-checked to see if her predictions were correct.

When Faith first started reading intervention, she demonstrated a lot of avoidance behaviors—making trips to the restroom, attempting conversations unrelated to the reading, saying she was not feeling well, putting her head down on the table. These behaviors were no longer an issue. By the end of our time together, Faith and I were meeting for thirty minutes a day, and she read most of that time and seemed happy doing it. Some days she was disappointed when she had to *stop* reading.

At the beginning of our time together, Faith had commented that reading was "sort of fun" but that she did not like to read more than she had to. In May, as our time was ending, she was saying that reading *was* fun and that she was reading more than her teacher required. She was engaging easily with text, and the tasks associated with her classroom reading assignments were less intimidating. She was willing to at least give it a go and do her best.

It was a gift to see Faith grow as a reader and a person. She was much happier, more relaxed, and less angry. Faith underwent a shift in her thinking about reading. When I asked her at the end of the year what she thought the most important thing about reading was, she said that "reading has to make sense" and "you have to think about what you are reading." Faith told me that she was "going to try to keep reading more," and I gave her books to take home with her. My hope for Faith is that she will keep reading—that she will become the reader she wants to be, the one we know she is capable of becoming.

See Figure 8 for a list of assessment tools and instructional methods I used to help Faith.

Figure 8. What Beth did to increase Faith's belief in herself as a reader (WM 2) and help her stay focused on meaning (WM 1).

Assessment Tools

Observation

Listening

Inquiry (asking questions to understand)

Dominie "Oral Reading Passages"

Modified miscue analysis

Systematic reflection on data using hypothesis–test process

Instructional Moves

Provided easy, high-interest texts.

Named and honored strategies used.

Encouraged synonym substitution.

Provided ample time for reading.

Provided books to take home.

Looking across Case Studies

The four children featured in the case studies—David, Rosalee, Joseph, and Faith—each received about five months (twenty weeks/one hundred days) of support from a reading interventionist across a school year. The majority of the children's time during their thirty-minute instructional sessions was spent reading.

The interventionists' classrooms are remarkably similar. They are all literacy-rich environments; every available space is filled with books. The classrooms range in size from "regular" (Beth's) to small (Lee's) to oversized offices (Kathy's and Anne's). Their rooms all contain a table and chairs at which they and up to four children can sit, a white or Smart Board, and chart paper on a stand. The larger rooms have couches and/or bean bag chairs.

All of the interventionists featured here collaborate with other members of the students' "teams," including classroom teachers, speech teachers, school psychologists, special education teachers, and the children's parents or guardians. (To ensure the anonymity of the children, this information has been omitted.)

Perhaps most important, all of the interventionists share a commitment to assessment as inquiry, to reflection on data, and to instruction that is focused on needs determined by assessment. In this way, all four reading interventionists live the assessment standards established by *Standards for the Assessment of Reading and Writing* (SARW) (IRA–NCTE Joint Task Force on Assessment, 2010). They all want their assessment(s) to "serve, not harm, each and every student" (p. 11). They therefore choose assessments that "emphasize what students can do rather than what they cannot do" (p. 11). When they ask students to read an oral reading passage from the *Dominie* (DeFord, 2004), for example, they choose passages that they know the students can read successfully. They understand that the point of giving the *Dominie* (or any other leveled reading passage) is not to "get" a level but to document the child's progress. To understand a child's progress, these interventionists observe, listen to children read on a daily basis, ask genuine questions, listen to children's responses, and reflect on all they have seen and heard. These informal assessments are "productive and powerful assessments" (SARW, p. 13) that "yield high-quality information" (p. 12).

These four teachers are the "primary agents, not passive consumers, of assessment information" (SARW, p. 13). They assign "meaning to interactions and evaluate the information that they receive and create" (p. 13). The teachers use the insights gained from reflection to inform their instruction. This rich description from the SARW captures the artfulness of these teachers:

Whether they use texts, work samples, discussion, or ongoing observation, teachers make sense of students' reading and writing development. They read these many different texts, oral and written, that students produce in order to construct an understanding of students as literate individuals. The sense they make of a student's reading or writing is communicated to the student through spoken or written comments and translated into instructional decisions. . . . (p. 13)

The result? After reading intervention, David, Rosalee, Joseph, and Faith felt better about themselves as readers and learners than they did at the beginning of the academic year. And they *were* better readers and stronger learners—they were better able to independently manage the text demands of the books they encountered in the classroom and the many books they will now choose to read independently.

Kathy, Lee, Anne, and Beth—like the other reading interventionists they work with and thousands of Tier 1 and Tier 2 teachers across the country—have chosen responsibility. In so doing, they have positively altered the academic and life trajectories of children. They are exemplars of our profession at its finest.

Note

1. The reading interventionists were Anne Downs, Jennie Goforth, Lisa Jaeger, Ashley Matheny, Kristi Plyer, Lee Riser, Beth Sawyer, Tara Thompson, Kathy Vickio, and Cindy Wilcox.

Classroom Portraits of Artful Teachers

s a teacher educator, I have long believed that preservice teachers would benefit if the first thing we helped them learn was
how to get to know one child. Every time I have that thought, I
am reminded of a 1984 column, "To Beth's First-Grade Teacher,"
that Dick Abrahamson wrote for the *Houston Chronicle*. In the current era, the
column may seem dated, but his point holds across time and audience. Writing
about how he felt as he and another father walked their daughters to their first-
grade classroom, Dick stated that he "didn't know the man in front of me that
morning. But I did notice that we both walked a little straighter, a little more
proudly, as our daughters held our hands" (p. 15). After leaving their daughters,
Dick Abrahamson wrote an open letter to his daughter's teacher:

> There were so many things we wanted to tell you, Teacher. Too many things were
> left unsaid. So I'm writing to tell you the things we didn't have time for that first
> morning.
>
> I hope you noticed Beth's dress. She looked beautiful in it. Now I know you
> might think that's a father's prejudice, but she thinks she looks beautiful in it, and
> that's what's really important. . . . I wonder if you noticed. Just a word from you
> would make that dress all the more wondrous.

Her shoes tell you a lot about Beth and a lot about her family. At least they are worth a minute of your time . . . solid, well-made shoes, not too stylish, you know the kind. What you don't know is how we argued about getting the kind of shoes she said all the girls would be getting. . . . In the end, she tried the solid blue ones and, with a smile, said she always did like strap shoes. That's the first born, eager to please. She's like the shoes—solid and reliable. How she'd love it if you would mention those straps.

I hope you will quickly notice that Beth is shy. She'll talk her head off when she gets to know you, but you'll have to make the first move. Don't mistake her quietness for a lack of intelligence. . . .

Did you know that Beth and her friends played school all summer in preparation for their first day? . . . Her play this summer was filled with positive reinforcement and the quiet voice of a reassuring teacher. I hope that her fantasy world will be translated into reality in your classroom. . . .

I did want to tell you about the night before that first day. . . . [After tucking her in], I gave her a kiss and started to walk out of the room. She called me back in and asked me if I knew that God wrote letters to people and put them in their minds.

I told her I never had heard that but I asked if she had received a letter. She had. She said that the letter told her that her first day of school was going to be one of the best days of her life. I wiped away a tear as I thought: Please let it be so. . . .

Well, Beth's first grade teacher, I think you're so lucky to have her as a student. We're all counting on you. Every one of us who left our children and our dreams with you that day. As you take our youngsters by the hand, stand a little taller and walk a little prouder. Being a teacher carries with it an awesome responsibility. (p. 15)

If preservice teachers saw each child the way Dick Abrahamson saw his daughter, they could approach the rest of their education classes knowing they were going to be responsible for supporting the learning of many wonderful, unique "childs." I would hope too that all inservice teachers take the time to really *see* each of the childs in their classroom. By emphasizing our responsibility to individuals—*to childs*—rather than to groups of children, we could fundamentally alter education in this country.

For classroom teachers, however, it is challenging to develop systems for getting to know every child. First, unlike the reading interventionists, they may be dealing with twenty or more children at any given time. Second, they do not have the luxury of daily small-group meetings with all of the students in their care. Third, they are responsible for multiple subject areas. Despite these challenges, many teachers have figured out how to teach a room full of unique "childs."

The eight teachers featured in this chapter have developed systematic ways to pay attention to each child—to get to know each and every one, both in and out of school—to know their families, their interests, their hopes, and their dreams. By assessing children in this way and then marrying assessment to instruction, these teachers are changing futures. In all of these classrooms, effective instruction begins with effective assessment.

The following portraits provide a close look at the tools teachers use to assess and document student growth and the subsequent instructional moves they make to ensure progress. In classrooms like these, more than 80 percent of students end the year reading on grade level and are therefore able to achieve the standards set for their grade. The teachers who help them do so are not only teachers of children. By example, they teach us all.

Preschool through Kindergarten

In early childhood classrooms, teachers are able to help children develop genera-tive theories long before the children make conventional use of print. They accom-plish this by reading to children and giving them time to read independently. They also provide students with time to write. All of these experiences provide children with the opportunity to learn that print is meaningful and pleasurable. Because they feel this way about print, they choose to read. If they did not see themselves as readers and writers before entering these classrooms, they become readers and writers in these classrooms—at ages three, four, and five. As part of getting to know each child as a reader, a move that for us is synonymous with assessment, teachers of young children talk to them, observe them closely, and create systems for keeping track of their growth.

Done well, this kind of assessment looks simple. It is, however, an art—one that is driven by a passion to know and support every child. The following three portraits detail this artfulness and illustrate how these teachers learn about their students. In the first portrait, Professor Julia López-Robertson and teacher Tammy Spann Frierson explain how Tammy learns about her preschool students through talk and story. In the second, classroom teacher Hope Reardon (writing in the first person, with Professors Diane DeFord and Lucy Spence) explains how she uses extensive informal and formal assessment in her kindergarten class for four-year-olds. In the final portrait, Professor Tasha Tropp Laman shows how classroom teacher Louise Ward uses observation and conversation to help her five-year-old kindergartners learn to read and write through writing.

Portrait 1: Tammy Yvonne Spann Frierson, Preschool Teacher

Julia López-Robertson with Tammy Yvonne Spann Frierson

Tammy and the Sensations: Assessing through Talking about Stories—A Preschool Approach

Background and Context

Tammy Spann Frierson has been a preschool through kindergarten teacher for sixteen years and has been at Spears Creek Road Montessori School in Columbia, South Carolina, for the past thirteen years. Located in a suburban area about twelve miles northeast of downtown Columbia, Spears Creek is part of Richland School District Two, the largest school district in the greater Columbia area. It serves about 25,000 students and is accredited by the National Association for the Education of Young Children. One hundred children attend the school, divided equally among the five multiage classrooms. The program for three- and four-year-olds is tuition based and the kindergarten is state funded. South Carolina ABC childcare assistance vouchers are also accepted for qualifying three- and four-year-old children.[1]

Tammy refers to the children in her classroom as "the Sensations—a beautiful eclectic group of nine boys and eleven girls who thirst for learning new things." The children range in age from three to five years old; eight of the children are kindergartners, five are four years old, and seven are three years old. Of the twenty children in the classroom, three are Latino, two are biracial (one is African American and Latina; the other is African American and European American), three are from India, seven are African American, and five are European American. The languages represented are English, Spanish, and Tamil. Whereas the diversity found in this classroom is representative of the population of South Carolina, it is unusual for diversity to be so well exemplified in one school.

Tammy knows that, in the United States, learning and schooling privilege some groups over others (Ladson-Billings, 1994; Nieto, 1999); therefore, she strives to make learning exciting and relevant for all her students. Because she believes that family is the child's first teacher and that a child's culture must be made part of the classroom, she invites families into the classroom to share their language, stories, and cultures. Families take advantage of Tammy's invitation and spend time in the classroom teaching about different cultures and languages.

Tammy not only learns about her children by talking with them, listening to them, and observing them, but she also learns about them through their families. Tammy's assessment tools are consistent with Standard 9 of *Standards for the Assessment of Reading and Writing* (SARW; IRA–NCTE Joint Task Force on Assessment (2010), which states that "assessment must be based in the local school learning community, including active and essential participation of families and community members" (p. 26). Tammy's ideas are supported by several researchers who urge teachers to use authentic assessment so they can learn about what children truly know (Owocki & Goodman, 2002; Ferreiro & Teberosky, 1982).

Learning with the Sensations

The heart of Tammy's classroom is a spacious multicolored carpet in the center of the room. The large blue section in the middle of the carpet is called "the ocean" and surrounding it are colored squares. Each child has his or her own spot on the squares; the ocean is reserved for Tammy and for group activities. The children know who all the squares belong to and they monitor this carefully. From their spots on the carpet, the children face the large whiteboard and the Smart Board, which are located at the front of the classroom. There is a chair next to the whiteboard where Tammy sometimes sits during whole-group instruction, although most days she can be found on the carpet with the children, figuring out mathematics problems, talking about current events, engaging in their unit of study, or telling stories. Next to the chair is a mini-sofa where the children sit when they bring in items for show-and-tell and read aloud to the class. Around the edges of the classroom are a computer area with three computers; an area for math exploration, full of math manipulatives and various types of puzzles; and a science area, anchored by a large fish tank. The children spend thirty to forty-five minutes a day working in these centers. The children gather at three round tables for writing or guided reading groups with Tammy or with the classroom aide, Mrs. Robinson. Mrs. Robinson and Tammy have been together for fourteen years and have their teaching routines down; they work completely in sync.

Tammy works with different groups of children at various times during the day. She groups them by age—threes, fours, and kindergartners. She also works with individual children throughout the day. She feels that grouping them by age allows her to focus on teaching the standards for that particular age group. She is especially concerned that the kindergartners leave her class well prepared: "I don't ever want any of my kids to feel unprepared when they enter first grade."

All of the children meet with Tammy and/or Mrs. Robinson daily for reading instruction; lesson length and format depend on the age of the children. The five-year-olds, for example, spend about twenty to twenty-five minutes in small reading groups, and they spend time individually with Tammy if they need more support with particular strategies.

During one-on-one time, Tammy focuses on getting to know the children as individuals—learning their interests, their family stories, and "what makes them tick." This, she says, provides her with ideas about units of study and helps her plan instruction to meet individual needs. In addition to the designated spaces already described, the classroom contains several areas for writing as well as bookshelves filled with a variety of children's literature. The children access books throughout the day and also have twenty minutes of free choice reading after lunch and recess; during this time, they read books from home or the classroom bookshelves. While the threes and fours take their afternoon nap, the kindergartners read alone or with a friend.

The day always begins as a whole group, with the children gathering at their spots on the carpet. The opening routine includes a variety of literacy-related activities. On the whiteboard is a list titled "Today's Lunch" with two columns that read "school lunch" and "lunch box." To the left of the list are dolls that represent each of the children. The felt dolls were created by the children; they bear each child's name. When the children come together in the morning, Tammy asks them, "What are you having for lunch today?" Each child walks up to the whiteboard when called, selects his or her doll, and places it under the appropriate heading: school lunch or lunch box. This informal assessment is part of the daily routine. The children must be able to recognize their name on the doll and be able to distinguish the difference between the words *school lunch* and *lunch box*. After the lunch count, Tammy usually reads aloud from a book related to the unit of study. She follows this by discussing the book and singing songs, which are written on chart paper. For example, one day when the class was studying life in the sea, Tammy read *Mister Seahorse* (Carle, 2004), followed by singing the song "Down by the Bay" (Raffi, 1987). This opening routine lasts between thirty and forty-five minutes. Afterward, Tammy tells the children what they will be doing next. They spend the following hour or so in small-group activities geared to their age group. On a particular day, Tammy might explain to the group, "I need my threes on the carpet for a math lesson, my fours up on the platform for writing, and my fives at the reading table."

Tammy has an engaging and calming manner with children; she is gentle but firm and knows each of the children well. She uses her knowledge of children to shape the curriculum. For instance, in the fall, while the other classrooms were focused on apples, pumpkins, and harvest, her students were particularly interested in birds. Instead of focusing on what the rest of the school was studying, Tammy followed the children's lead and started a month-long study of birds. Tammy wove assessment into this study and used it to guide instruction. One morning, when the children were all gathered around the carpet attentively listening and quietly focused as Tammy read *Amazing Birds* (Kindersley, 1990), she stopped reading and asked the children to remain silent for a few minutes to let the information "sink in." There was total silence for a good two minutes—anyone who has been in a preschool classroom knows that this is not an easy task—before Tammy said, "So, we heard a lot of information on this page. Do you have any questions? I know I have some. Mrs. Robinson, do you have any questions? You know what I am going to do? I am going to write down your questions right here on our whiteboard." One by one, the children raised their hands and asked their questions or gave comments: "How do birds poop?" "What color are their eggs?" "Why are there so many seagulls in the parking lot at Target?" "Why is bird poop white sometimes?" "What do they eat?" "Do all birds eat mice and squirrels?" Tammy repeated each question or comment as a way to double check that she understood what the child had said and as a way to gauge the speaker's recollection of what he or she had said. She then wrote the comment or question on the board. When their discussion was finished and the board was full of questions, Tammy told the children how impressed she was with all the information they knew about birds and invited them to follow along with the pointer and read the list with her. Then she asked, "How are we going to find out all these answers?" A kindergartner's hand shot right up: "Mrs. Frierson, we can go on the computer!" and another child said, "We can read more books."

The kindergartners had been with Tammy for three years; they knew exactly what was happening—Tammy was introducing their unit of study. From that discussion, the children conducted individual and group research, which involved books and the computer and taking notes on the information they found. All the children took notes as appropriate for their age—some drew their notes and, with their teachers' help, labeled their illustrations; others used a combination of drawing and writing. All used invented spelling. The children then met every morning as a class to share what they had found, raise questions, and read more books about birds. These whole-class meetings served as an informal assessment that provided Tammy with "a quick look" at what the children were learning. While the children shared, Tammy took anecdotal notes; later, she met with them individually or in small groups to address any inconsistencies and provide missing information.

All of Tammy's units of study end with some kind of project showcasing what each individual child has learned. One day toward the end of their bird study, for example, Tammy was on the carpet with all of the kids listening to them talk about birds:

> Okay, we have spent about a month learning all about all kinds of birds. I learned things that I didn't even know about birds! Here is what we are going to do. You are each going to pick a bird that you like and think is cool, and then you are going to do some research. You will go on the computer with a grown-up and find out some facts and write them down for us, look at some books, draw some pictures, and then share it with all of us. Now, my kinders, you know that your parents can't do any of the writing or drawing, it's all you. I want it on a nice poster so that we can all see your beautiful work and hear about all of your information. I will get this out to your families this afternoon. I think this is going to be fun! What do you think?

Because of the enthusiasm with which Tammy explained this assignment, all of the children were excited to start their bird projects. Based on the initial research they did as a class, each child selected a bird to study independently. Some of the birds chosen were hawks, parakeets, vultures, and chickadees. The project requirements differed by age: the threes drew and labeled pictures with help from their parents; the fours drew, labeled, and wrote some information with a little parental help; and the kindergartners drew, labeled, and reported specific information about their particular bird with little, if any, help. Each child then presented his or her poster and reported the information to the class. By following the children's lead, Tammy was responsive to their particular curiosity about birds and was able to capitalize on their general interest in science. Tammy explained that through these types of projects she was able "to learn what each of the children learned. I am not giving them tests; the projects are pretty open-ended, and I get a lot of information back from the kids."

Children's Talk as a Means of Assessment

A lot of time in this classroom is spent talking—about current events, stories, and the unit of study and while playing. Tammy values this talk because, as an experienced early childhood educator, she knows that children's talk "is a window into their knowledge and thinking" (Owocki & Goodman, 2002, p. 49). Tammy uses student talk in several ways. First, she uses it to assess their engagement. When students talk through their thinking without being prompted, she knows they are meaningfully engaged. On the other hand, a lack of talk suggests that she hasn't provided a significant or engaging task, or that her students don't see the task as important. Second, Tammy uses talk to assess understanding. When students produce seemingly abstract pieces of work, they also explain their work. In this way, Tammy gains insights into their thinking. Third, the constant dialogue in the classroom allows Tammy to diagnose and supportively address learning issues as they arise and before they become what others might describe as "deficiencies" in her "little people." In addition to assessing naturally occurring student talk in these settings, Tammy holds intentional conversations with children that allow her both to assess and to teach.

It's All about Comprehension

When it comes to reading, Tammy believes that comprehension is the most important element for her to focus on with her multiage students. As she explained, "Many times they can read the words easily, they have figured out how to decode, but if I ask them *what* they read, they have no idea. This doesn't help anyone. They have to know what they read or what I am talking about." Through talking and informal assessments, Tammy determines whether the children understand that reading is about comprehending.

Tammy often crafts stories to get the kids thinking about real life in order for them to make sense of the book they are talking about. For example, when a child was reading a book about a missing dog and Tammy wanted to ask the child how the characters found the dog, she began with "I lost my favorite cup the other day when I was at home. I couldn't find it anywhere and I was so upset. Then my husband walked in and I said, 'James, have you seen my cup, you know my Carolina cup I use to drink my water?'" Then she asked the child, "What did I do to find my water cup?'" The child responded, "You asked Mr. Frierson for help. That is the same thing that they did in the book, they asked somebody else for help!'"

Tammy's conversations with children are simultaneously teaching and assessment moments. Her questions send the message that reading is about making sense, that the children are capable readers, and that reading is pleasurable. At the same time, Tammy is able to use what she learns from the children to make curricular decisions. For example, to help the children understand the significance of what she means by "understanding what you read and hear," she told them the story of the missing keys:

> I left Mrs. Robinson a note on my computer and it said, "Mrs. Robinson, don't lock the door. I can't find my keys and I won't be able to get back in." Well, Mrs. Robinson read my note; she said every word nicely and pronounced each letter just right (you know Mrs. Robinson knows how to read). But you know what? She locked the door! So now I ask you, what happened? Mrs. Robinson read my note; she knew what all the words said and told me every letter on the note, but what happened?

The children raised their hands wildly and called, "I know, Mrs. Frierson, I know what happened!" Tammy asked a couple of the kids to explain; one said, "She read it and didn't get it." Others added, "Mrs. Robinson reads in Spanish not English," "She was busy and didn't have time to remember what the note said," and "The words didn't make sense to her, so she needs to read it again so it makes sense. Right, Mrs. Robinson?" Tammy accepted all their ideas and added, "'The most important part of reading anything is understanding what you read. It isn't going to help anyone if you know all the letters and words but don't know what they mean. See what happened to me—I got locked out!" In this exchange, Tammy helped the children understand what reading is, and she gathered information about what each child already understood. Tammy often holds such whole-group conversations; she also makes ample time for one-on-one teaching–learning conversations.

Listening to and Learning from Michael

Michael is a four-year-old African American boy whom Tammy has known all his life. This is his second year in her class; his brother, Mason, also spent three years in her class. On this particular day, once all of the other children were working independently in centers, Tammy casually invited Michael to "talk about a story." Michael had not yet chosen to read independently; he read only when asked to and, while he always followed along when a peer read, he had not yet shown any interest in deciphering words or pictures. Instead, he focused on the social aspect of sitting with someone while they read him the story. During reading choice time, Michael often could be found enjoying books with his classmates. This indicated to Tammy that Michael understood reading as meaningful and pleasurable and that reading was "coming" for Michael.

As Tammy started walking toward the table where she would sit with Michael, she was interrupted by several children who exclaimed, "Mrs. Frierson, I want to talk about a story!" She happily responded that right now it was Michael's turn and reminded them that everyone would have a chance later to talk to her about a story.

Tammy and Michael comfortably settled at a table, sitting next to each other with their bodies turned so they could see each other. Tammy opened with a casual, "Michael, how are you doing today?" to which he responded, "Okay." Tammy then offered, "I'm working on a story and I want you to tell me if it's any good. I need you to listen and tell me what you think. Do you want to hear it? Can you help me?" Michael nodded and Tammy then said, "Okay, once I am done, I am going to ask you some questions so you can tell me about the story. Okay, ready?" She read the story while Michael listened carefully.

After she finished the story, Tammy asked Michael to tell her everything that he remembered about the story. Michael began to retell the story and stopped at one point and said, "I don't think that I remember anything else. That's it." Tammy asked him a couple of detailed questions, but Michael showed no interest, so she moved on. Tammy later explained to me that she had chosen a story about a dog because Michael loves *Clifford the Big Red Dog* (Bridwell, 1963), and it is always best to begin with the child's interest because "I get more out of them when they care about the story."

In what follows, Tammy was trying to gauge Michael's interest in books—trying to see what he was interested in reading. She began with a story:

> I was at Books-A-Million the other day. You know I like to read and I was looking for a book to read. Have you been in that store? You know it's big? So I was walking around looking at all sorts of books and couldn't decide on one. Finally someone that works there came up to me and asked me what kind of books I like to read; she was trying to help me find one. I told her what I liked and then she led me to the aisle and I found a great book. Michael, do you like to read books?

Michael (M): I like Harry Potter.

Tammy (T): You read Harry Potter?

    M: At summer camp.

    T: You enjoy books being read to you? I know you do, because when I read at school you always listen.

    M: I found a book about cars.

    T: Can you tell me about your favorite book? I like *The Napping House* [Wood, 1984].

    M: *Go Dog Go!* [Eastman, 1961]. That's the book I like.

    T: Yeah, I've seen you reading it. Michael, what do authors do?

    M: They write the words.

    T: What about the illustrator? Do you know what the illustrator does?

M: No.

T: I'll tell you what they do—they make all the pretty pictures in the books.

M: I see all those pictures on my computer and on my brother's [Nintendo] DS. I have a game with a lot of cars.

T: I have seen you reading books about cars here in school. Michael, let me ask you one more thing and then we'll be done, okay?

M: Okay.

T: I forgot my glasses today and I am trying to give Mrs. Robinson this list of words, but I don't know what it says because I can't see them. Can you help me figure them out?

M: Okay, I will help you!

T: Thank you, Michael. Here we go.

[Michael reads the words on the list, which were from the story he had just heard.]

T: Michael, you know that I am very proud of you. I needed help reading these words and help with my story, and you did such a nice job helping me. Thank you.

M: You are welcome, Mrs. Frierson. If you need more help, let me know.

Tammy began the assessment by inviting Michael to talk about a story with her; his subsequent retelling of the story indicated that he was able to capture the main idea of the dog story. This helped Tammy assess whether Michael understood that reading meant making sense of text. She combined what she observed with her other observational data and concluded that yes, he did understand this. She then conducted a mini-interview that also began with a story so that she could share her interest in reading and find out what books Michael liked to read. She was able to elicit that Michael listened to J. K. Rowling's Harry Potter series while at summer camp and that he liked to read about cars. Although he said that he didn't know what an illustrator did, he was able to make a connection to the pictures he saw on his computer and his brother's Nintendo DS. This confirmed for Tammy that Michael was a "thinking" listener. Tammy's assessment ended with Michael successfully reading a list of words that were drawn from the story. This provided Tammy with data showing that Michael was making connections between what was read and what was on the page and that he had a strong visual memory.

Tammy values what she learns about her students from these story talks. She noted that by telling the children stories about things that interest them, "I really get to know what they understand and what they are thinking about." She added, "If they don't like a story, they don't seem to listen as much."

Listening to and Learning from Parents

To learn even more about her students, Tammy periodically sends questionnaires home with the children that ask family members to provide her with information that will help her be a more effective teacher. Sample questions include: *What is your child interested in? What does your child like to play with? What kinds of print materials are available in your home? What language(s) are spoken in the home? What would you like your child to accomplish this year in reading?* Tammy uses the responses along with what she learns from the children themselves "to create meaningful conditions for learning" (Owocki & Goodman, 2002, p. 23) for each of the Sensations. By using information from questionnaires, from parent–teacher conferences, and from talking with families when they drop their children off in the morning, Tammy is able to craft units of study that are of interest and relevant to her children. For instance, while talking with one of the fathers at drop-off time, Tammy found out that he was an assistant football coach at a local university. She and the children were all excited to learn this, since all were fans of the team. Everyone became even more excited when they learned that they were going on a field trip to the football stadium and that they might meet some of the players. Tammy planned a unit of study around this event, which involved learning the names of some of the players, estimating the length of the football field and how much time it would take to run from one end to the other, and making thank-you cards for the student's dad. The unit was relevant to the children and their families, and each of the children was actively engaged.

Learning across Assessments

Tammy recognizes the importance of using assessments, both formal and informal, as tools to inform her teaching and to provide her with a more complete picture of her students. She merges data from more formal reading assessments, the district's Dynamic Indicators of Basic Early Literacy Skills (DIBELS) and the Developmental Reading Assessment (DRA), with her informal assessments—observing, talking, listening. Then, by involving the families in the process as "active, essential participants in the assessment process" (SARW, p. 29) and using that information to build her curriculum, Tammy has multiple data sources she can draw from, which is consistent with the SARW's Standard 8: "The assessment process should involve multiple perspectives and sources of data" (p. 24). Tammy ends with a more complete picture of each of the Sensations and, as a result, is better able to teach them and "improve the quality of teaching and learning" (p. 16).

Through her artful use of assessment tools and instructional moves, Tammy is helping these three-, four- and five-year-olds develop a generative theory of reading. By reading to them, talking to them about books, and giving them time to read and talk with one another about books, she provides them with the opportunity to learn that reading is a meaning-making process, that they are readers and members of the literacy club (Smith, 1987), and that reading is pleasurable. She also helps expand their oral vocabulary so that when they begin to conventionally read they will be familiar with an academic register and the types of words found in books.

See Figure 9 for a list of the assessment tools and instructional methods Tammy uses in her classroom.

Figure 9. Classroom teacher Tammy Spann Frierson's assessment tools and instructional moves.

Assessment Tools

Observation

Listening

Inquiry (asking questions to understand)

Interviews

Storytelling with retell

Word lists

Parent questionnaires

Developmental Reading Assessment (DRA)

Instructional Moves

Read aloud.

Provided time for independent reading.

Provided time for writing.

Created authentic opportunities to use reading and writing.

Asked questions based on meaning.

Provided mini-lessons about reading as meaningful.

Wrote songs on chart and referred to it during singing.

Modeled fluent reading.

Let children know she believes in them as readers and writers.

Crafted curriculum tied to student interests.

Portrait 2: Hope Reardon, 4K Teacher

Hope Reardon with Diane E. DeFord and Lucy K. Spence

Support and Engagement in a Kindergarten for Four-Year-Olds (4K)

I (Hope) teach four-year-old children in an urban school that is tucked within a small neighborhood. The school's 388 children are 85.3 percent African American. The poverty level is high, with 86 percent of the children receiving free or reduced price lunches. My classroom is made up of thirteen African American, five Latino/a, and two European American children, all of whom receive free lunch. At the beginning of the year, the school screens all children using the *DIAL-3: Developmental Indicators for the Assessment of Learning*, Third Edition (DIAL-3; Mardell-Czudnowski & Goldenberg, 1998). This is a three-part early childhood screening for language, concepts, and motor abilities. The school uses the results to place children in my 4K child development class. Last year the DIAL-3 screening assessment identified twelve of my twenty students as being at risk, or below the 33rd percentile. At the end of the year, the children are given this same assessment to document progress and growth and to make decisions about student placement and services.

Throughout the year, I use informal checklists, kidwatching notes (Goodman, 1978; Owocki & Goodman, 2002; Whitin, Mills & O'Keefe, 1991), photographs, and video to document learning. Six different times during the year, I use the "Inventory of Letter Knowledge" from the *Dominie* (DeFord, 2004). In January, to assess the children's knowledge of print concepts, I use the "Show Me Book," also from the *Dominie* (DeFord, 2004). I purposefully use observation of students as an ongoing form of assessment within my classroom. I am constantly taking notes about my students as they interact with one another within instructional engagements (learning centers, journal writing time, read-alouds, etc.). By combining notes, photographs, work samples, and the assessment tools I used to guide my observations, I have an ongoing record that provides me with different sources of information from which to determine the strengths and needs of the students I teach. This information influences my teaching and allows me to document the progress of each child. I use these ongoing observations, informal assessments (including running records, teacher-made inventories, writing samples, and anecdotal records), and district standardized tests to help me devise lessons, craft new experiences, and gather additional resources so that all of my students can develop as well-rounded readers and writers.

As a 4K teacher, I believe that my responsibility is to offer the richest literacy experiences possible to support children's development. I target key interventions as necessary, focusing on what children show me they know, not what they don't know. I believe strongly that "assessment should emphasize what students can do rather than what they cannot do" (SARW, p. 11).

I use data from these informal and formal assessments to plan small-group and classroom instruction. I structure flexible small groups in this classroom; groups change almost weekly based on particular skills and strategies for which I've identified a need. In the classroom, I take anecdotal notes as the children work in their different learning centers. I use these notes along with more formal checklists to help inform my small-group instruction. For example, the children love to play with magnetic letters on a cookie sheet. As they play and make words, we discuss the different letters they are working with. This informal assessment helps me truly understand whether the children are still struggling with certain letters or if they have mastered letter knowledge. Another favorite is the big book center. When the children read in the big book center, I note the print concepts or strategies they use when they play "teacher." While the children rest each day, my assistant and I discuss our observations of the children. I use these conversations to plan future small-group instruction. This practice is similar to one established for other emergent literacy settings that use flexible, small-group interventions for the youngest students (Scanlon & Anderson, 2010).

I have taught for fifteen years, including four years as a literacy coach. To help me conceptualize my constructivist, child-centered classroom, I draw on the scholarly writing of Cambourne (1995), Vygotsky (1978), Harste (in Harste, Woodward, & Burke, 1984), Halliday (1969, 1973), Genishi and Haas Dyson (2009), and Paley (1981, 1990). In my classroom, the children have hundreds of books to read and a variety of writing tools. I put books in all of the centers. I label classroom items and display environmental print. To personalize the room, children also bring material from home. I help the students use these tools and use language (spoken and written) as the medium of exchange for ideas, discoveries, questions, problems, and solutions.

In my class, children engage in meaningful learning; there is a purpose for everything they do. They never do mindless busywork. When they receive letters in the classroom mailbox, they see a purpose for writing letters. They eagerly read their mail, write letters back to their friends, and "mail" them. My teaching assistant, Tina, and I accept the children's approximations as they make marks to represent writing. I expect all of my students to become readers and writers by the end of the year. I plan ways for them to use and practice new learning, and I provide feedback as they take their next steps. I make time for them to talk about what they are learning, and I take the time to listen and respond.

My classroom curriculum is based on children's interests and what they want to learn. I embed key skills into each experience. At the beginning of the year, I make home visits to find out more about the children and their families. For example, one little boy loved dinosaurs, so I made sure to have dinosaur books and toy dinosaurs in the block center. To help build a sense of family in our classroom, we begin the year with games from *The Peaceful Classroom* (Smith & Downing, 1993). I encourage talk and sharing. In this socially active community, it is the children themselves who welcome visitors and new children into their classroom family. My teaching assistant and I plan and work together to facilitate children's learning within this classroom. Throughout the day and within instructional engagements, informal assessment guides my instructional decisions.

Informal Assessment across the School Day

Beginning the Day

Tina and I greet the children as they arrive in the morning, unpack their bags, and pick out new books to take home. They sign their names in the daily sign-in book and begin independent reading time with books from their individual book bags.

Independent reading is not a quiet time. Children gather in small groups on the carpet with their reading pillows to laugh and talk about their books. They also read their favorite shared reading books together. On Friday, at the end of independent reading time, they look for books for the next week for their book bags. They have the option to keep books they have in their bags or get new ones. Their favorite books and the new books their friends like are quickly snapped up.

This morning routine is a key time for me to take note of several things. I pay careful attention to how the children sign their names, as this helps me understand their developing understanding of concepts about the letters that constitute their names. I listen when children talk to one another and use language to express ideas. I notice what books they choose and I think about their interests so that, as needed, I can suggest new titles.

Morning Meeting Time. After independent reading, the children gather as a family for morning meeting time. They notice if any of their friends are absent and send good thoughts out the window for the absent child. Music and movement are a part of all activities during this time. I project many of the children's favorite stories or songs on to the Smart Board so they can follow the printed text as they sing. Morning meeting ends with an interactive read-aloud projected by a document camera. I always have a planned read-aloud, based on a unit of study or author study, but if the children have a request, Tina or I will read it. Tina uses different voices while reading aloud to the children and they love that.

I watch how engaged the children are with the different books, what they respond to, and how their use of "book language" is coming along. Do they repeat refrains? Do they use the pictures? Do they offer up connections they are making between their lives and the information in the book and pictures? Do these book themes, characters, and the language of books find their way into center and play times?

Center/Work Time. Center time is an hour of free exploration and activity for the children. The learning centers all feature books, pictures, and print to support the activities and children's learning. These are the traditional centers you will find in any early childhood classroom: housekeeping (based on themes or seasons), blocks, painting, sand and water table, art center (markers, stamp pads, alphabet stampers, play dough), math center, flannel board center with cutouts made from shared reading books, puzzles and games, reading center with a large collection of books and pillows, puppet center, Smart Board, computer center, and a writing center with a variety of writing materials.

Center time follows High Scope's Plan, Do, and Review framework (Hohmann, Weikart, & Epstein, 2008), in which the children plan their center time with an adult. The children then work and play independently in their chosen center. Afterward, they talk with one another about what they did. During center time, when I gather children for small-group instruction, I integrate my observations and assessment information into the lessons, and I note additional information about student-initiated activity. Are students using literacy experiences purposefully as they work and play together? When I expose them to new ideas, or practice something with them that we have worked with before, are they incorporating what they've learned?

Writing Workshop. Writing workshop begins with a mini-lesson of a skill or strategy, modeled on the interactive whiteboard, with the child or adult talking as he or she writes. Then the children go off to write in their journals. The adults in the room move from child to child to talk about each child's individual writing and to write comments on sticky notes placed in the child's journal. At the end of writing workshop, I ask a child or a volunteer to share the writing with the class. Two to three children share their writing each day. The author asks for "questions and comments" from the audience, and I record the author's responses. I scan the children's writing into a document so I can write their words as they share, and we videotape these sessions. Toward the end of the year, the children's writing from the previous day becomes the mini-lesson for the day. I invite the author to come up and tell about her writing and what she might change or add. Sharing is the highlight of writing workshop time for the children. My notes about their application of skills and strategies as they write and talk about their writing, as well as the video and writing sample records, are a key part of the assessment data I use to follow children's progress in writing, social interaction, language use, and how concepts of print are being applied as they write and then further discuss their writing with others.

Shared Reading. During shared reading, we all enjoy reading and rereading big books and poems. (The children especially love hearing the same text read again and again.) If a particular big book is not available, we use the document camera instead to project the text onto the board.

During this time, Tina or I model particular concepts of print. When possible, I find an audiobook or a version of the story that is set to music so the children can hear the text in other formats. I create cards with pictures so the children can retell or sequence the story in a pocket chart. To aid story retellings, I make flannel board pieces to accompany the picture cards. I also create character name and picture "vests" for the children to wear as they act out the stories. After we read the books and then work with sequencing cards and flannel board pieces, we place these materials in a center so the children can revisit the story during center time.

I am particularly interested in seeing how children's life experiences and their new literacy learning experiences are being integrated. Because many of these four-year-olds are just now being introduced to the world of books, numbers, print, formal educational practices, structured play, and self-initiated, school-based activity, I can use my notes, classroom artifacts, photographs, video, and informal and formal assessments to judge the effectiveness of my teaching and how children are adapting to these experiences.

Math Time. Our math time usually begins with a picture book that is based on a math concept. We read many math books by Stuart J. Murphy (e.g., *Double the Ducks*, 2003). After the read-aloud, the children and I model what to do with the math materials, and the children then go off to practice. After math they have free exploration. During this time, Tina and I take note of who was not yet able to complete the task independently, and we place these children in small flexible groups for more practice.

Recess and Lunch. Recess is free exploration outdoors. We play racing games, dig in the wood chips, and play on the tricycles and playground equipment. Sometimes this play turns into a spontaneous group game. For example, after reading *The Three Billy Goats Gruff* (Galdone, 2008) during shared reading, I observed the children using the bridge on the playground to retell the story, with one child under the bridge and other children "stomping" over it.

Ending the Day

Near the end of the day, the children rest on mats and listen to soft music. This quiet time begins with reading aloud *Sleepy Bears* (Fox, 2002), using the children's names in the story. As I read, I walk around the room and stop at the child whose name I add. Once I read their names in the page from the book, the children almost always close their eyes. They seem to wait until they hear their name read aloud. At the end of the story, I walk around again and wish "sweet dreams" to each child. A few months before the end of school, instead of reading *Sleepy Bears*, we read from chapter books, beginning with *Charlotte's Web* (White, 1952/2004). Once the children wake up, they pack up their folders and eat a snack. After the snack, they read books until their bus or their parents arrive. They choose favorite books that we read during the day or books I've made multiple copies of so that they can read side by side with their friends and family. I take this opportunity to meet with individual children and read with them, chat informally, and talk about their school day.

My philosophies about assessment and instruction inform my decisions about teaching whole groups, small groups, and one on one. The case study that follows details what this looks like up close. The informal and formal assessment data I collected on Democlease, a child who struggled with learning to read and write, were an important source of information the school needed to make decisions about what additional resources to employ in this child's literacy education.

Assessment and Instruction: The Case of Democlease

Democlease was one of the lowest-scoring children on both formal and informal assessments. In terms of formal assessment, on the DIAL-3 100-point scale, Democlease scored a 2 at the beginning of the year. At the end of the year, he scored 34, just above the 33 percent cutoff score. Ongoing classroom assessments show that his knowledge seemed to ebb and flow across the year (see Table 3).

Democlease joined our classroom at the end of October as a quiet and reserved child. As with many new children, he mostly watched and listened. I soon learned that his maternal grandmother was raising him (he referred to her as "Mom"). After two weeks in the classroom, I noted a change in Democlease's quiet, watchful attitude during our shared reading of *The Little Old Lady Who Was Not Afraid of Anything* (Williams, 1986). When the children began to clap, stomp, nod, and wiggle, for the first time Democlease actively joined in. For the next two weeks, when we read this story, the children wanted to act it out using character vests. Democlease wanted to be the little old lady—and he made an awesome one.

Democlease seemed to blossom socially as we read and reread this book. He started smiling and talking with the other children and built some important new friendships. When we celebrated him as the main character in *The Little Old Lady*, he grew in confidence. I also witnessed Democlease singing songs and stories that were set to music. Observing Democlease in this rich literacy environment allowed me to get to know him as an individual and fueled my reflections, decisions, and instructional moves. As the SARW suggest, this observation "provide[d] useful information to inform and enable reflection" and "yield[ed] high-quality information" (p. 12).

My observations also led me to see changes in Democlease during center time. At first he chose solitary activities, but within a month he began playing

Table 3. Informal Assessment Results (Democlease)

Time of assessment	Colors	Shapes	Number recognition	Counting (up to) without missing a number	Uppercase letter recognition	Lowercase letter recognition
October	2/10	3/8	0/21	5	0/26	0/26
November	5/10	2/8	1/21	9	0/26	0/26
January	2/10	2/8	0/21	11	0/26	0/26
February	7/10	3/10	0/21	9	1/26 (E)	0/26
March	2/10	3/10	0/21	6	0/26	0/26
May	6/10	2/10	1/21	12	3/26 (D, G, Z)	1/26 (u)

blocks with the other children. He also began talking to children in the housekeeping center as they took turns playing the mother or the father. He loved dressing up and often fought over the little pink poodle skirt. When we made the housekeeping center into a costume shop, Democlease found the cups and tray that I had put away. He donned the apron and started "serving" the children who sat at the little table outside the center watching the fashion show. Democlease became very inventive with materials in his environment and used them to create new stories and act them out with other children. This helped him integrate socially into this new classroom and engage more actively with others. In the puppet center, for example, he often grabbed a friend to scrunch down below the screen, open the curtains, and "pop up" with the puppets. Democlease also liked to use flannel pieces in the flannel board center to tell his favorite stories.

In November I administered the "Inventory of Letter Knowledge" (DeFord, 2004) and could see the impact these social interactions and classroom experiences had on Democlease's literacy learning. He associated certain letters (*U, M, S, B, V, D, A, N*) with the letters in his name and the names of his friends. For example, for the letters *S, B,* and *D,* he said, "That's my name." For the letters *U, M,* and *N,* he said, "That's Mohammad's name." For the letter *V,* he said, "That's Victor's name," and for the letter *A,* he said, "That's De'Aja's name." His morning sign-in sheet showed he was not yet using letters in writing his name, but he did separate drawing from writing and wrote about meaningful events in his life. In a sample from his journal on November 17, Democlease attached a word card. What I found interesting was that he used the word *family* and drew a family. Vygotsky discusses this very shift in learning:

> There is a critical movement in going from simple mark-making on paper to the use of pencil marks as signs that depict or mean something. All psychologists agree that "the child must discover that the lines he makes can signify something." (1978, p. 113)

These informal teacher tests and formative assessments, such as letter knowledge and book handling assessments, provide critical information that helps me make instructional decisions. As noted in the SARW, such "formative assessments that occur in the daily activities of the classroom" are "the most productive and powerful assessments for students" (p. 13).

Democlease needed to learn more about letters, colors, shapes, numbers, and concepts about print. So, with information gathered from an alphabet assessment, the "Show Me Book" from the *Dominie* (DeFord, 2004), and observations during shared reading and writing workshop, I developed focused small-group lessons. We played games with letters, objects, and different shapes; read a lot of predictable texts; and, while reading, reviewed the print concepts we were working on during shared reading. To help with his emerging math concepts, we counted out objects and worked on creating patterns. To help him learn the letters in his name, we formed letters with play dough and Democlease wrote letters and words in shaving cream.

Occasionally I worked more closely with Democlease on the letters in his name in one-on-one time. He made his name with magnet letters, wrote it in shaving cream, and then wrote it on paper. As we worked with these letters, we talked about them and made connections between the letters in his name and things that were meaningful to him. For example, he loved to eat Doritos, so he knew that his name started just like the word *Doritos*. These one-on-one interactions involved a lot of talking, writing, and reading predictable texts—texts we created as a whole class as well as stories Democlease wrote in his journal and for which I provided the conventional spelling.

In addition to the daily homework folder, Tina made file folder games (letters, shapes, and numbers) for several of the children to take home. For Democlease these folders included the letters in his name and several differently colored shapes. The instructional goal for Democlease was the same as for all children in terms of literacy learning: to use literacy in a variety of settings and to learn more about literacy through reading, writing, talking, and listening. As part of the children's daily homework, they picked a book from the classroom library to read at home with their families. The children knew they could pick any book they liked. Sometimes the book they chose was one of the stories we had read aloud the previous day; other days it was a book from their individual "just right" reading bags. In the beginning of the year, we held a parent workshop on reading with your child during which we modeled with the children an interactive read-aloud and showed the families how they could involve their children in the reading of the text. In the part of the weekly newsletter where we shared with families our shared reading story, I also included the current concept about print skill we were working on and gave the families tips on how to work on this skill at home with their child.

Democlease's oral language, self-confidence, and literacy knowledge increased throughout the year. He moved from being a silent child to one who talked freely with others—one who was interested in reading and in what others were doing. Still, at the beginning of March, I remained concerned with his letter and number recognition. When he picked a word card for writing workshop and I asked him what the word was and which letters were in it, he was unable to tell me. During our morning meeting, when we talked about a friend's name and the letters that make up the name, he still could not tell us the letters in his own name. The informal letter and number assessment that I complete on each child throughout the year confirmed my observations from writing workshop.

I could have arranged for Democlease to receive supplemental services, but I decided to keep him in the regular classroom environment and increase my interventions with him. I felt I knew him better than anyone else did and that I could help him learn more about the print concepts we were working on in shared reading; I was confident that I could use his small-group time to really focus on the skills he was still struggling with. Because I understand that children grow and develop at different rates, I was hoping that Democlease was a "late bloomer"—just like other four-year-olds I had seen in the past—and I believed that it was still possible for him to catch up. I decided to request a meeting with our school's support team to discuss my concerns. At our school, the principal, school psychologist, special education teachers, and classroom teachers meet formally at the request of a classroom teacher to discuss and offer suggestions and support for students whom the teacher is concerned about. In March, I requested one of these meetings to discuss Democlease's particular needs. The meeting would not be held until the following fall, which gave me plenty of time to collect the required six weeks of data.

By May, Democlease was able to identify three uppercase letters (D, G, Z) on a letter identification test and u in the lowercase set. This score placed him in the 2nd stanine, or low-achievement band (see Figure 10). By contrast, the letter knowledge of the two other children whose literacy learning I had worried about had escalated (the mean was 24.7); 57.8 percent of the remaining children were in the average or high-achievement bands (stanines 4–9) on the "Show Me Book" from the *Dominie* (DeFord, 2004), which measures a student's knowledge of book handling, including identifying the title. Democlease scored five out of seventeen (which is in the 2nd stanine) on turning pages, finding the print on the page, etc. He knew where to start reading, he could locate the first and last letter of a word, and he could find the word "*no*" on a page of the book. The majority of children in the classroom also could identify these concepts. Most of the children could also read and write their first name, demonstrate left-to-right directionality of print, and return to the next line of text. Democlease could not.

When I checked on Democlease the next fall, his kindergarten-for-five-year-olds (5K) teacher said he struggled at the beginning of the year with letter knowledge but had learned his colors, shapes, and numbers up to ten. Democlease moved from our school at the end of February, in his 5K year. At that time, he knew all of his letters and was beginning to read very easy, predictable books from the district reading series.

This story of Democlease demonstrates how young children emerge into literacy in my classroom. I believe all children need a rich literacy environment in which to learn. They need opportunities to talk and learn through play and through involvement in authentic literacy experiences. Although district-required assessments were necessary to place children in my class, and uniform measures were needed to track children's progress across classes and schools, individualized, formative assessment was the most useful in helping children make progress as

Figure 10. Concepts of written language.

Concept	Known by >50%	Democlease's Score	Known by <50%
Write first name	61%	0	
Write last name		0	28%
Read name	56%	0	
Start left page	94%	1	
Start right page	94%	1	
Matching one to one		0	17%
Left to right directionality	83%	0	
Return to next line	61%	0	
Locate one letter		0	33%
Locate two letters		0	22%
Locate one word		0	11%
Locate two words		0	11%
Show first letter in a word	94%	1	
Show last letter in a word	61%	1	
Locate the word *yes*	50%	0	
Locate the word *no*	61%	1	
Read "I like to read and write"		0	0%

readers and writers. Without the ongoing observation and analysis I do throughout the day and across weeks, I would not be able to design effective instruction that takes into account children's individual strengths and needs. The key to good teaching is for teachers to be artful kidwatchers—to notice what children can do, what they can almost do, and what new learning may be difficult for them. All of this must be contextualized to inform me about how classroom engagements stimulate these children to learn. Every teacher must take the time to talk with children, to discover each child's thoughts and interests. With this information, teachers can effectively support the learners in their classrooms.

See Figure 11 for a list of the assessment tools and instructional methods that I use in my classroom.

Figure 11. Classroom teacher Hope Reardon's assessment tools and instructional moves.

Assessment Tools

Listening

Inquiry (asking questions to understand)

Daily sign-in sheet

Teacher-made checklists (numbers, counting, shapes, colors)

Photographs of writing samples, center work

"Inventory of Letter Knowledge"

"Show Me Book"

Dial-3 (Beginning and end of year)

Creative Curriculum Work Sample Assessment (Fall, Winter, and Spring)

Reflection

Instructional Moves

Created extensive classroom library.

Put books in all the centers.

Labeled classroom items.

Displayed environmental print and materials from home.

Created classroom mailbox.

Accepted approximations.

Expected all children to be readers and writers.

Made home visits.

Embedded skills into authentic experiences.

Integrated children's interests into curriculum.

Encouraged talking and sharing.

Created checkout system for books that go home each night.

Provided time for independent and paired reading.

Put stories and songs on Smart Board.

Used document camera for interactive read-aloud.

Used reading and writing workshop curricular structures.

Met with children in flexible small groups based on need.

Portrait 3: Louise Ward, 5K Teacher

Tasha Tropp Laman with Louise Ward

Writing in Support of Reading: Teaching into Agency

Twenty-two kindergartners who attend an urban school in the southeastern United-ed States sit on a large alphabet rug at the front of their classroom. The children in this kindergarten class resemble the diverse racial and cultural demographics of their school, where 55 percent of children receive free or reduced lunch and where more than fourteen languages are represented. Their teacher, Louise Ward, points to the morning message written on the whiteboard. It contains blank spaces. As she and her students read the message aloud, Louise calls on the children to fill in the blank spaces, using their growing repertoire of reading and writing strategies.

> Morning Message
> Hello, Amigos,
> Today is _ebruary 23rd. We will learn _____ things in math measurement. We also
> _____ music _____ library.

Louise:	Eleanor, what is missing in the first blank?

[Eleanor writes a capital *F* on the whiteboard.]

Louise:	Let's look at what Eleanor wrote. Why do we need a capital?"
Thomas:	[raises his hand] It is at the beginning.
Louise:	[gently] Let's look. It isn't at the beginning of the sentence.
Thomas:	Because it is in the middle!
Louise:	[smiles] Do you want to get a friend to help you?

[Margaret whispers to Thomas.]

| Thomas: | Because February is a name. |

[Louise then goes to the next sentence and the children read together, "We will learn some things in math."]

| Louise: | I'm going to underline some parts of this word [*measurement*] and maybe we can say it. |

[She underlines the *m*, *s*, *r*, *m*, and *t*. The children slowly say the sounds and then say "measurement."]

| Louise: | You used clues you know to sound out that word. That was a BIG deal, kindergarten. Kiss your brain. |

[Louise then has the children fill in the two remaining blanks with the words *have* and *and*. She then points to the words *where*, *house*, *cat*, *am*, and *tree*, which are written on the whiteboard below the morning message. She calls on Alex to read the word *where*. Alex does not reply.]

Louise:	This is a question word. It is the /wh/ sound and the *r*. Does anyone have another way to help Alex know this word? Don't tell him. Help him.
Sophie:	Where.
Louise:	Say it loud now. Alex, say the word. What does the word *where* mean? Look at me, because you want to learn that word. Alex, where are you?
Alex:	School.
Louise:	When I ask, "Where?" I want to know a place. *Where* are you going after school? If I ask, "Where you are going?" you would tell me the name of a place.

Similar morning message routines are repeated daily in early childhood classrooms across the country. These brief messages offer children a forecast for their school day—glimpses of what they will study, think about, and experience. Many teachers, like Louise Ward, see morning message time as an integral part of reading instruction. Through daily messages, teachers can highlight text and print features within an authentic text and reinforce key concepts about print such as sound–symbol relationships, punctuation, and spacing. Morning messages also give children the opportunity to see high-frequency words.

Although these morning message routines may be familiar to many educators, what I am always drawn to as a researcher in Louise's classroom is the language she uses inside of structures like morning message to support and get to know children as readers and writers. Louise sees assessment as extending power to her students so that they become agents of their own learning. Johnston (2004) contends that language is the tool of our teaching, emphasizing:

> Teachers' conversations with children help the children build the bridges between action and consequence that help the children develop their sense of agency. They show children how, by acting strategically, they accomplish things, and at the same time, that they are the kind of person who accomplishes things. (p. 30)

Whether she is teaching calendar math or holding reading or writing conferences, Louise is constantly assessing for understanding through her questions, comments, and observations. She tailors her teaching to each child and emphasizes students' participation in talking about their thinking and their learning—offering students agentive positions. She understands, after thirty-seven years of teaching, that assessment is both highly interactive and ongoing. In her exchange with Alex, Louise slowed down the quick review of high-frequency words to make sure that Alex and everyone else on the floor understood the word *where*, which will appear throughout their reading lives. In my observations of Louise and my talks with her about her assessment strategies, she emphasized that she:

> feel[s] obligated to know that [the children] truly understand what I am teaching. It always runs my lessons long because I have a drive to help them understand. It takes extra time. When I realize that they don't understand something I want them to understand, when they aren't answering a question, I want them to know that it isn't just about answering the question that I am asking. I want them to be able use the tool [that I am teaching]. There is power in that. I want *them* to have the power. I don't need it.

Louise embodies the SARW. She knows that her questions and her students' answers are neither right nor wrong. Instead, she views her teaching as part of a bigger picture. She understands that, by highlighting the thinking behind her actions and interactions, she raises her teaching to a metacognitive level. Because of this, she is able to help her students learn to use the tools and access the power of learning and literacy. She helps them own their learning.

Louise is like all busy teachers; she gets to work early and stays late. She continually has questions in mind about her students' literacy learning and what she expects children to develop during their kindergarten year with her:

> What's helping them understand the text? Are they reading the pictures? Can they read patterned books? Are they using text and beginning sounds? I want them to understand they can stretch out a word from beginning through the middle and to the end. I notice the words they are using all the time in their writing.

Like all great teachers, Louise also knows that each child has unique needs. When I ask her what she looks for in children's writing, for example, she says:

> It depends on the child. Can Dawson get his ideas down without me next to him? For Celina, I want to see her try what I taught in the mini-lesson. For Kyra, I want her to ask herself, "Is there something I need to fix up or fancy up?"

During the day, Louise writes anecdotal notes about her students that will jog her memory in the evening. And every evening she writes reflective notes about the day (see Figure 12). Louise's notes are rich resources that she uses to direct her instructional decision making. Assessment, then, informs her instruction. The children know this and often leave her little notes about things she needs to remember the next day. In this way, Louise uses assessment to extend power to her students.

Louise began teaching within a writing workshop structure five years ago as a second- grade teacher. Writing workshop provides multiple opportunities for authentic assessment and responsive teaching. It supports both readers and writers and makes assessment highly personal and interactive (SARW, Standards 3 and 5). Louise considers writing workshop a transformative part of her professional development. Her students produced stronger writing and were more engaged in writing and reading when she taught relevant mini-lessons, conferred with writers during independent writing time, and asked them, during share time, to reflect on what they had learned about themselves as writers. Children who were often reluctant to read began initiating their own reading and made more progress than in years past. When Louise moved to kindergarten, she was committed to using writing workshop with her new, younger students.

Writing workshop positions her kindergarten students in powerful ways. Louise has noticed that the children are interested and motivated when they write about things that matter to them. They want to read their own texts and the texts generated by their friends. What they learn as writers helps them as readers. As writers, children learn that texts make sense, that they carry meaning. They also learn that they can write and read and that texts are pleasurable. In this way, writ-

Figure 12. Sample of Louise's reflective notes.

| Cumulative Writing Record for ~~████~~ | | | School Year 2011–12 | |
Date D/W Book or Booklet Topic/Title	Knows About Craft (sense of story, organization . . .)	Knows About Conventions (spelling, punctuation, etc.)	Needs to Learn	When to Teach
Raccoons 2-13-12 3-8-12 3-14-12 Non-fiction writing	• Interested in nonfiction writing • effective use of anchor charts independently • Notices nonfiction craft in other books • illustrations match writing • relates his writing to what is happening in his world	• listens to sounds in words independently but often hear sounds incorrectly "hudrs" for hunters "taxts" for tracks • includes vowels in most words	• blends tr (tracks) (trees) • endurance for working independently w/o teacher approval/help • writes minor backwards <u>liat</u> for tail in diagram occasionally	• WS – focus on (blends) • IW – focus on tr • ML – model my story and wanting to share it before it is complete
Poetry 3-19-12 3-27-12 I Want a Pet Lion Monster Trucks My Toys My Dad Golf	• Very receptive to writing form • Does not use shared writing poem topic but takes something from his knowledge • Writes at least 1 poem a day • easily thinks of topics	craft • picks up forms of other poems read during ML • poems easily read with creative spelling gofo = golf pakds = practice	some • poems still written in sentences ↳ can be ok depending on how it is written on page • uses X for s sound at end of Trucks = trucakx Doesn't understand ⑤ means more than one.	• WS – small group • ML – model other kid writing • IW –

ML= mini-lesson   IW = interactive writing   Conf = conference   RA = read-aloud   Conv = conversation   MM = morning meeting   WS = word study

Talking, Drawing, Writing: Lessons for Our Youngest Writers. Martha Horn and Mary Ellen Giacobbe. Copyright © 2007. Stenhouse Publishers.

ing helps the children build a generative theory of reading. Children bring these understandings to the stories they read in class. They expect books to make sense, they expect to be able to make sense of books, and they enjoy reading. From writing, children also learn how texts work—that they have a beginning, middle, and end; that sentences can continue on another line or another page; that pictures help tell stories, etc.—and this helps them better understand the texts they read. In addition, writing provides an opportunity for the children to learn about sound–symbol relationships. They pay close attention and take an inquiry stance toward letters and sounds because they want to communicate a message to others. Phonics knowledge, then, is useful to them, and the knowledge they gain about it as writers helps them as readers to problem-solve unfamiliar words they encounter in their reading.

In the following transcription of a writing conference, zoom in on the moment-to-moment teaching and interactions that occurred on one day in Louise's writing workshop. This mini-lesson and the ensuing writing conference provide a lens into what it means to teach young readers and writers. Notice how Louise continually assesses her students as she teaches toward reading and writing competence. Notice also how she positions her students through her language in agentive ways that ask the learners to talk through their thinking. The skills and ideas she highlights are those she wants her students to carry with them throughout their lives.

On this February day, more than halfway through the academic year, Louise gathers her twenty-two students on the large alphabet rug in the front of the room. She sits in her white rocking chair, ready to begin the day's mini-lesson. She uses her anecdotal notes as a launching point:

Louise: Who can tell me what we have been doing in writing?

Sarah: Writing about a moment in our life.

Louise: What moment have you written about?

Jackson: Soccer, getting a pumpkin.

Louise: Yesterday I was reading your stories and I noticed you are doing lots of smart things. We have been stretching our stories. What do we want to add?

Alex: Words!

Louise: [Louise takes out Sophie's book and holds it up for the students to see.] Look what Sophie did. I am not going to say anything. You tell me what she did. [Louise slowly turns the pages of Sophie's book.]

Student:	Shows pictures!
Student:	Showed details.
Louise:	She did show details in her pictures.
Gerald:	She drew before she wrote.
Louise:	Is that a good idea? How does she know what she wants to write about? She drew the pictures. She knows what happened first and next and last.
Louise:	[to Sophie] Can you tell us what you want to add to this page?
Sophie:	We are going to see my grandma.
Louise:	Could you tell us how? We want to see those details. Then what happened?
Sophie:	She was excited.
Louise:	What do you do when you see your grandma?
Sophie:	Sometimes we eat her blueberry muffins and play with her doll-house!
Louise:	[to whole class]. Do you remember the story I told you about the fire drill? Remember, we have to have details. You are doing a great job. I want to know all the little details like Sophie just shared about the blueberry muffins and the dollhouse. Today I will be at table 3. Remember, we are working on beautiful pictures and great stories.

Louise's mini-lesson draws on what she knows about the particular children in her room, literacy theory, and how children learn through authentic literacy practices. She moves seamlessly between teaching readers and teaching writers. She tells her students that they have been learning to stretch stories across many pages, just like writers do. When Louise shares Sophie's writing with the children, she is showing them that authors add details to help their readers. She is putting meaning first.

Writers hold a vision of readers in their minds when they construct texts, and Louise reinforces this idea throughout the mini-lesson. All year she has taught her students to "see" images when they read. In the mini-lesson, she makes it clear that these five-year-old writers also need to help their readers see the details of their texts.

Louise fills the mini-lesson with assessment and instruction. She begins by making a connection to the children's ongoing writing work. She reminds the children about what they have been doing—stretching a story across many pages by adding details. Louise makes clear that she is an interested reader—she takes their writing home at night and reads it; she notices and remarks on their growing repertoire of writing strategies.

Louise then holds Sophie's writing up for all of the children to see. She slowly turns the pages of the book so that the kindergartners can see what their fellow classmate has done. Louise doesn't talk. The children share what they notice about Sophie's latest book—that she "shows pictures" and "shows details." Because Sophie's book is unfinished, Louise asks Sophie, "Can you tell us what you want to add to this page?" This is a powerful question. Louise is clearly positioning Sophie as the author of this text—the only person who can determine what goes next. She expects that Sophie will have an answer to her question. Louise does not leave it there. She asks Sophie questions to elicit more words from Sophie, such as the details of her story (and the focus of the mini-lesson). These details are just what the children have talked about all year as readers. They are now learning how to craft the kinds of texts rich with details that will create pictures in their readers' minds. Louise ends the mini-lesson by reiterating her teaching point, that writers add details through "beautiful pictures" and "great words." Implicit in this lesson is the understanding that readers expect details from authors.

After the lesson, the children gather the books they are making and return to their tables. Louise joins table 3 to conduct individual writing conferences. She starts with Aisha:

Aisha: [holds her book with white stapled pages and tells Louise] I'll read it to you. "When I first saw Santa Claus. I was . . . ." [Aisha gets stuck at the word *thirsty*, and Louise slowly moves her finger under the word and helps her remember the word.]

Louise: Do you remember what you wanted to say?

Aisha: I wanted some water.

[Louise nods in agreement. Then, because she has noticed that Aisha has run out of room on the page for her writing, she asks] Do you remember what you can do if you run out of room on the page?

Aisha: I can turn the page and add my words.

Louise: What can you do? [Coaches Aisha in a soft voice as she turns the page] Add your *I.* Authors work hard to make an *I*. Will you make it little or big? Remember, we always make *I* big when we write it by itself.

[Aisha erases everything on her page and then writes, *I got some water.*]

Louise: Is it okay to stretch your words across to a new page? It is a very grown-up thing to do. You are doing such big thinking. Let's go back and read it.

Aisha: [reading the text] "When I first saw Santa Claus I was thirsty so I . . ." [Aisha then turns the page over and writes *got.*]

Aisha: Um um [as she slowly says "some"] "Wa-wa- wa-ter."

Louise: Is that the end of your sentence? So what goes there? [Louise then reads] "When you went to get some water." You just wrote a beautiful sentence. What was your next thought?

Aisha: "I saw him." Capital *I?*

Louise: Yep. That is the next thought in your beautiful head.

Aisha: [writes "hem" for *him* and says she needs to sharpen her pencil] I'll be back as soon as I can. [She returns and writes *i* in *him.*]

Louise: Where did you see him? [Santa Claus]

Aisha: At my Christmas tree. [Says "Christmas" very slowly] "C-r tree." I already knew how to spell it.

Louise: Give me five. That was a complete thought.

Aisha: He shhh me. [Puts her finger to her lips.] He shushed me and I went back to bed.

Louise: [giggles and repeats] He shushed you.

Louise: *I.* What did I tell you about *I?*

Aisha: Capital *I.* [Looks at the word wall for the word *went.*] That is all I can think of! I'm out of ideas!

Louise: Let's read the whole thing. I want you to try to write very clearly so I can read it. I read late at night so I need help seeing the words clearly. What is your next job?

Aisha: Draw pictures.

Louise: You want to draw. The illustrator's job is hard too because they have to look at the words first then draw the pictures. What will your first picture be?

In her content and coaching conference (Anderson, 2000) with Aisha, Louise continually shifts the focus of her teaching between reading and writing. For example, in line 2 of the conference, she asks Aisha what she wants to say next in her writing. She makes it clear to Aisha that Aisha is the only person who knows her story and what she wants to say. This teaching move may seem insignificant.

It is not. Its importance lies in how Louise positions Aisha and makes identities available to her. Every time Louise says, "What did *you* want to say? What will *you* do next?" she puts Aisha in an agentive position as an author—someone who is capable of writing, telling stories, and creating texts that are relevant to *her* life and that others want to read. In line 8, Louise identifies Aisha's understanding about stretching text across multiple pages as "big thinking" and "a grown-up thing to do." This understanding will help Aisha as she reads more complex texts in which words and ideas extend across pages.

Louise's words gesture toward the big ideas of literacy: "Writers make decisions, writers write from their lives, writers know what to do when they run into a problem and are able to solve it. Writers are strategic." Similarly, at every turn Louise demonstrates how texts work. She asks Aisha, for example, to punctuate her sentences and reminds her that stories contain "complete thoughts." As Louise works with Aisha, she makes notes—ideas and insights—that will inform her reflections later that evening. Most notably, she records Aisha's newest growth—her understanding that, when all of her words do not fit on one page, she can carry them over to a new page.

Some researchers have argued that writing should be taught before reading because the very act of writing demands meaning-making (Chomsky, 1971; Elbow, 2004; Bomer, 2007). Elbow (2004) reminds us that nothing can be read unless it was first written, and Bomer (2007) suggests that we cannot ignore the teaching of writing because, for some children, "writing leads" (p. 151) their literacy development. Thus, reading and writing are interrelated and interdependent processes. Children engage in similar practices whether they are reading or writing (Harste, Woodward, & Burke, 1984). Writing instruction is therefore inseparable from reading instruction. As shown in this interaction, Aisha, as a reader and as a writer, is steeped in learning letters and sounds (phonics) in the context of her own messages because it matters to her that her audience understand her. And the same is true for reading. Aisha is also learning about how books work. Louise shows Aisha how to take text onto a new page. This is an important understanding for young readers who may have, thus far, read only books in which each page contains a single sentence or idea and limited vocabulary. At every turn, Louise demonstrates how texts work. She does this when she asks Aisha to punctuate her sentences and reminds her that stories contain "complete thoughts." And she does this when she asks Aisha to read the finished text, a completed book that will entertain Aisha's classmates and delight her family.

Now that Aisha understands how to stretch a story across pages, she is also prepared for books she will encounter when she is reading independently, as well as positioned to notice more about the books that Louise reads aloud—books that use rich language, varied sentence structure, and complex story lines. This constant movement between reading and writing supports Aisha as a person who is learning to make meaning as she reads and constructs texts.

After twenty-five minutes of independent writing time, the children gather back on the carpet for share time. Louise holds Aisha's book in her lap.

> **Louise:** I want to share one thing today. I was working with Aisha and she did something so smart. [Louise holds up Aisha's book and slowly turns the pages.] What did Aisha do first? This is something exciting. I don't know if anyone has done this yet. See if you can see it. [Louise slowly turns the pages again and begins reading.] "When I first saw Santa Claus I was thirsty so I got some water. He shushed me so I went back to bed." What did she do?
>
> **Brandi:** She took one page and didn't finish it and stretched it to another.
>
> **Louise:** Exactly! You can do that too when you are writing and you run out of space; you can turn the page to add your words to the next page.

Share time is an important space for noticing and naming (Johnston, 2004) what children do as writers and how that writing work is related to reading work. Louise does not use this time to have every child read his or her writing, though there are days when children do share their most recent publications. Instead, during share time Louise may ask children to share something they tried that was new, and she will record this sharing to document the student's growth. On this particular day, Louise chooses to elevate Aisha's work by marking it as a landmark learning moment. Louise says, "I don't know if anyone has done this yet," which documents an understanding of this class' collective growth as writers. Just as she did in the mini-lesson, she uses the children's writing to showcase an example of literacy growth and development. This time Louise highlights Aisha, who wrote her words before adding illustrations, which is a different writing move from the one she highlighted in the mini-lesson, where the child author drew her pictures before adding words. This deliberate teaching move demonstrates for children that there are multiple ways to write texts—you can start with pictures or you can start with words.

Louise's success across all of these settings (morning message, independent writing time, writing conferences, and sharing sessions) is due in part to her way of being with children—she creates a warm, supportive academic environment in which children are helpful to one another; she actively encourages reflection and helps develop agency by asking questions that only the child can answer; she answers children's questions; she names their strategic moves; and she responds as a reader and a writer to their literacy work. Most important, Louise is a deliberate and diligent teacher who pays close attention to her students and uses what she knows about them to refine her instruction. Because of this, she succeeds in having a positive impact on children and their literacy development. This kind of artful teaching shapes children's literacy learning in Louise's kindergarten classroom today and provides a strong foundation for her students' lives, filled with learning literacy and making meaning.

See Figure 13 for a list of the assessment tools and instructional methods Louise uses in her classroom.

Figure 13. Classroom teacher Louise Ward's assessment tools and instructional moves.

Assessment Tools

Listening

Observation

Inquiry (asks to understand)

Anecdotal notes

Reflective notes (based on data Louise brings home)

Children's notes

Instructional Moves

Created morning message.

Conducted writing conferences.

Designed and carried out mini-lessons.

Modeled thinking.

Named children's strategic moves.

Coached during composing.

Focused on meaning.

Encouraged reflection.

First and Second Grade

In first and second grade, some children already have a generative theory of reading, and teachers help them hold on to and deepen that theory. Other children do not yet have a generative theory, and their teachers help them build one. In most elementary schools, first and second grade is a time when children are expected to be able to independently and conventionally make sense of print, aka "be able to read." To help children reach this goal, their teachers carefully and systematically gather data that help them form hypotheses about every child as a reader. While continuing to focus on meaning and agency and to emphasize reading as pleasurable, they collect data about the reading processes of each student. This is often a collaborative process. In Ryan Brunson's first-grade classroom, Ryan collaborates with her literacy coach, Kristy Wood, and the reading interventionist, Susie Laffitte. Together they collect and analyze data and use it to make curricular decisions. University faculty member Pamela Jewett visited with this team and worked with Ryan and Kristy to tell their assessment story. In Tim O'Keefe's classroom, Tim explicitly collaborates with the children. He is assisted by Heidi Mills, a university faculty member who, along with Tim and others, started their school; she serves as curricular facilitator. In the portraits that follow, both teachers foreground one student to show how their collaborative problem-solving and instructional sessions ensure that all students grow as readers in their classrooms.

Portrait 4: Ryan Brunson, First-Grade Teacher

Pamela C. Jewett, Kristy C. Wood, and Ryan Brunson

No Such Thing as Perfect: The Need for Multiple Assessments and Assessors

We—classroom teacher Ryan Brunson, literacy coach Kristy Wood, and university faculty member Pam Jewett—all recognize that there is no such thing as perfect where assessments are concerned. Each assessment procedure has its own limitations and biases, sometimes favoring one student over another. The need for multiple indicators is particularly important in assessing reading and writing because of the complex nature of literacy and its acquisition. A single measure is likely to be misleading or erroneous for individuals or groups. For example, assessing students who are new immigrants to the United States by asking them to read a book about a culturally specific topic like the Fourth of July would not be a fair assessment, nor would it help us understand how they might read other texts. Instead, to better understand students as readers, we need to collect data from multiple sources.

We also believe that there is no such thing as a perfect assessor. Our beliefs about assessments and assessors are best reflected in Standard 8 of the SARW, which states that the assessment process should involve not only multiple sources of data but also multiple perspectives. We acknowledge that our perspectives about what it means to be a teacher or a literacy coach influence how we interpret assessment data. For example, two educators with different points of view on literacy might describe data about the same student in very different ways. However, exploring these different perspectives through dialogue, with all of its meaning-making potential, may enrich our understandings of a student's development and broaden possible interpretations. This belief in multiple assessments and assessors plays out most noticeably in our school's Student Growth Meetings, in which several educators meet to evaluate student growth. In the following exchange, excerpted from one such meeting, Ryan, Kristy, and Susie Laffitte, the school's reading interventionist, met to better understand Evan, a first-grade reader:

> **Kristy**   [speaking to Ryan and Susie]: In our Student Growth Meeting today, I want to begin with the conversation we started in study group and look at Evan, a student who both of you [Ryan, as his teacher, and Susie, as his interventionist] work with. I went ahead and looked at his latest *Dominie* [DeFord, 2004] text reading level assessments [oral reading passages], and I want to begin with sharing what I noticed based on analysis of data, and then I want to spend time comparing this to what you are seeing daily in your classroom.

> **Ryan:**   Good, because the other day in the Student Growth Meeting, when we began analyzing Evan's data, a teacher said that, based on his text reading assessment, it looked like he doesn't know high-frequency words. I question that observation because in my classroom he seems to have a good core of sight word knowledge in isolation. What I think is that he doesn't use those words in reading.

Even in this short excerpt, we can see how these teachers valued multiple data sources in understanding students' learning and held multiple perspectives for analyzing and interpreting the data they collected. By talking about data from formal and informal assessments, they came to understand the theories of reading that Evan held and then used this knowledge to plan instruction that would help Evan develop a more generative theory about reading. Meetings like these are one way to honor the teachers' beliefs about multiple assessors and assessments.

In this portrait, Kristy and Ryan explain their stances toward assessment and how immersing themselves in multiple assessments affects coaching and teaching at their school. Pam then discusses what assessment looks like in the same school from an observer's perspective.

In Kristy's Words: Taking an Inquiry Stance toward Literacy Coaching

Ben Hazel Primary is a rural K–3 school with 56 percent European American students, 41 percent African American students, and 3 percent classified as "unknown." Fifty-six percent of the students are eligible for free or reduced lunch. The faculty hold weekly study group sessions to support our growth as professionals and weekly collaborative planning sessions about "how" we teach. However, we strongly believe that we must also have structured time to focus primarily on children. To create this time and space and to keep student growth at the heart of our thinking, we conduct weekly Student Growth Meetings. In these meetings, multiple assessors come together to evaluate student progress.

We schedule these meetings so that different groups of teachers meet on alternating weeks (see Figure 14). During the meetings, regular school volunteers come in and take each class to recess and lunch so teachers are available to meet and discuss the students they have concerns about. Each teacher brings artifacts to share with the team, and someone records the session. Typically, the teachers, literacy coach, and administrator are involved in every meeting. Other teachers, such as interventionists, attend if schedules allow.

To guide the Student Growth Meeting, teachers complete a planning sheet beforehand, which gives them an opportunity to think about their students before the meeting (see Figure 15). On the planning sheet, teachers explain their areas of concern, what evidence they have related to the concern, and what actions students take (if any) to problem-solve. At every meeting, we address a series of guiding questions, including:

- Are there different approaches the student/teacher could use to problem-solve?
- What are ways to teach for alternative approaches?
- Do you need to collect more data? What data do you need?
- What resources are available to help?
- What are some structures/ways to hand over control to the student?

In a two-week cycle of action and reflection, on the week teachers do not meet, they have time to implement what was discussed at the meeting, reflect on student progress, gather and analyze further data, and plan for interventions and the next Student Growth Meeting.

As a school, we agree that "seeking multiple perspectives and sources of data . . . takes advantage of the depth of understanding that varied assessment perspectives afford and the dialogue and learning they produce" (SARW, p. 25). Data collection is followed by reflection. The give-and-take of talk between team members

Figure 14. Schedule for student growth meetings.

	Ben Hazel Primary School Student Growth Meetings 2011–2012	
Schedule		**Expectations**
10:05–10:40 Kindergarten	****Every Monday****	◡ **FOCUS—** Reading/Writing
10:45–11:20 1st Grade	***Meetings will be held in the**	◡ Each teacher will bring artifacts from one student to share with team.
11:35–12:05 2nd Grade	**Data Room****	◡ One member each week will act as the recorder for the session and complete the documentation form.
12:20–1:00 3rd Grade		◡ The purpose is to support growth in **ALL** students—high and low performing.
		◡ Any teacher who didn't get to share their student during the meeting will share the next session.
		◡ Begin the next session with a follow-up on student progress and instructional strategies from previous meeting.
		◡ **Stay on task and use a timer!**

brings our multiple perspectives into a cycle of data collection, reflection, and planning.

I have been a coach or consultant since 2006, and before that I was a K–4 teacher for eleven years. As a coach, I find that taking the time to sit down with colleagues to talk about children, share data, and reflect together is extremely helpful in moving students forward. The act of slowing down, noticing and naming,

Figure 15. Planning worksheet for student growth meetings.

Student Growth Meetings—Planning Worksheet

This section to be completed prior to Student Growth Meeting.

What is the area of concern?

What is the evidence (data)?

What independent actions does the student take to problem-solve?

Guiding questions to be discussed/documented during Student Growth Meeting:
Are there different approaches the student/teacher could use to problem-solve?
What are ways to teach for alternative approaches?
Do you need to collect more data? What data do you need?
What resources are available to help?
What are some structures/ways to hand over control to the student?

---

and looking across multiple assessments from various contexts is powerful—and one of the most important ways we support one another and our students. Working with others not only helps us see students from different perspectives but also allows us to become more intentional in our support of these children. For example, some of our students receive reading support/intervention from various teachers, and they often get mixed messages across these learning contexts. Therefore, when all teachers work together, we create a common language and a shared focus for our students. One way we've found to help create that commonality is through a shared framework for assessment and subsequent classroom strategies.

Framing Our Assessment Work

In this excerpt from Jon Muth's (2002) picture book *The Three Questions*, the main character, Nikolai, seeking to be the best person he can be, asks his mentor, Leo, these universal questions:

Nikolai: When is the best time to do things? Who is the most important one? What is the right thing to do? . . .

Leo: Remember that there is only one important time, and that time is now. The most important one is always the one you are with. And the most important thing is to do good for the one who is standing at your side. For these, my dear boy, are the answers to what is most important in this world. (Muth, 2002, n.p.)

As a literacy coach, much of my day revolves around similar questions that lead me to better understand the teaching and learning of the teachers and students I serve: Could it be? Did you notice? Can you tell me more?

I believe that inquiry is at the core of real understanding; it is the heart of authentic assessment. As a literacy coach, I too seek understanding. Living in the moment and being aware of those around me are powerful guides for "doing good"—for improving the practices of teaching and learning. I believe that good teaching is reflective teaching—really "looking closely and listening carefully" (Mills, O'Keefe, & Jennings, 2004) to the children that you teach. To me, this is the true purpose of assessments.

However, I have found that without some type of framework, assessment becomes the end of the road instead of the beginning. Assessments, then, tend to focus on what students struggle with instead of where their strengths lie. In our study groups, we have read about assessment from many practitioners (e.g., Hindley, 1996; Hubbard & Power, 1993; Rasinski, Padak, & Fawcett, 2010; Routman, 1996; Taberski, 2000). Of those, I have found Johnson's (2006) assessment framework to be particularly teacher-friendly. It was included in professional development courses taken by many interventionists and became the model that I suggested for our school (see Figure 16). Johnson's framework became the basis for our Student Growth Meetings and is at the heart of our conversations about how to be intentional with our teaching and move students forward.

My role is to create such opportunities for teachers and interventionists to come together with a common language and plan to help students succeed. Whether it's during Data Days, when we spend time in vertical and grade-specific teams analyzing data from various formal assessments such as the *Dominie* (De-Ford, 2004), or through classroom observations that focus on informal assessment procedures such as questioning, response strategies, observations, anecdotal notes, running records (Clay, 1993), and miscue analysis (Goodman, Watson, & Burke, 1987), the teachers and I continue to ask those three important questions: "When is the best time?" "Who is the most important one?" "What is the right thing to do?"

Figure 16. Johnson's (2006) assessment framework.

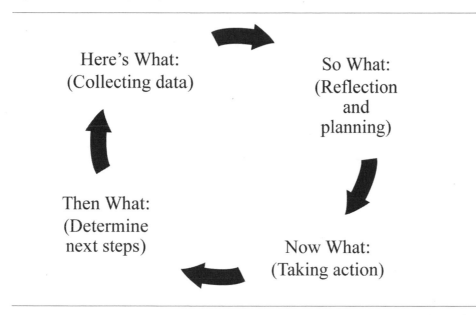

In Ryan's Words: Formal and Informal Assessments and Learning from Tests and Talk

As a classroom teacher, I too believe in situating assessment in multiple perspectives and data sources. I have been teaching preschool through first grade for eleven years, the last nine of them at Ben Hazel Primary School. I strongly believe that instruction begins with the individual first graders in my classroom. I use a variety of tools to assess areas of strengths and places where students may need support. I believe that the "reliability of interpretations of assessment data is likely to improve when there are multiple opportunities to observe reading and writing" (SARW, p. 25). Three times a year, I use the *Dominie* (DeFord, 2004) to document my students' abilities with sentence writing and spelling, text reading levels, and core reading words. As I learn more about each student, I am able to differentiate instruction to meet all of their needs. For example, in my guided reading groups, I incorporate reading, writing, and word study and then differentiate based on what the next step would be for each group. One group might work on comprehension, another on word work strategies to attack unknown words, and yet another on increasing fluency through readers theater.

Although I conduct ongoing informal assessments such as running records (Clay, 1993), observations, anecdotal notes, and over-the-shoulder miscue analyses (Davenport, 2002), I also believe in talk as a significant way to learn from and about my students. It is one of the primary forms of ongoing, informal assessment in my classroom. Talk is an important way for students to share what they know with me. As we move through a balanced reading curriculum, I learn about my students through their questions and comments. For example, we hold story time each day. I read chapters from books such as those in Mary Pope Osborne's Magic Tree House series, and I encourage my students to "turn 'n talk" (Harvey & Goudvis, 2007) about the story. Their talk gives me a window into their thinking and helps me understand the knowledge they are building from the reading about the story content, plot and characters, and craft of the author. I use what I learn to focus my support.

I do not, however, want to be the only teacher in my classroom. I believe that my students should also be teachers. Because I believe that learning is a social practice, my classroom is full of spaces for students to support one another through talk. They gather at tables, on rugs, at the Smart Board, at kidney shaped tables, and in cozy, defined reading areas. I encourage them to share their learning with one another. They readily confer when they are in literacy centers, reading big books, reading the room (with pointers and flashlights), reading in the book nook, and also when they are writing responses to literature in their journals. For example, one of my students tried to spell the word *Australia* in his response journal and could not figure it out. He conferred with his neighbor, who reminded him that he could go look on the globe, and together they found it.

From Pam's Perspective: Layers of Assessment and Assessors

As an observer in Ryan's classroom, I can see that the assessment–assessor environment is complex. Ryan creates multiple layers of formal and informal assessments to better understand her students' learning and shapes instruction to support them. She is familiar with the various types of formal assessments (such as district and state evaluations) and informal assessments (such as running records, observations, and anecdotal notes). And she is cognizant of the multiple assessors at her school site who collaborate to assist her in assessing her students' literacy learning. Despite all of this, Ryan clearly believes that it is not mandatory that assessments be designed by professional educators, nor must assessors always be classroom teachers, literacy coaches, or interventionists. She honors this belief by providing space and time in her classroom for students to learn with and assess one another as they confer about their learning in spaces such as literacy centers, book nooks, and writing centers. In the case Ryan described earlier, in which one student helped another determine how to spell *Australia*, these two students—in thoughtfully crafted learning environments—assessed their knowledge and inquired together to find an answer. Ryan also uses the classroom learning environments she creates to listen carefully to her students' talk, believing that it is "a window into their thinking" and another source of assessment data for her. In Ryan's first-grade classroom, there is an ongoing and integrated spiral of multiple assessments that are interpreted by multiple and multiaged assessors. The following case study is an example.

Inquiring about Evan: Cycles of Multiple Assessments and Multiple Perspectives.

Student Growth Meeting. Learning more about Evan as a reader started with a Student Growth Meeting. The meeting included Kristy, the literacy coach; Ryan, his classroom teacher; and Susie, the reading interventionist. The literacy team met to better understand what was happening as Evan read. Evan was currently meeting the criteria for a *Dominie* (DeFord, 2004) Level 3B, which at that point in the year meant he was reading below grade level. He was not successful at the next benchmark. His accuracy at Level 3B was 92 percent, his fluency was three out of four, and his comprehension was 100 percent. Based on their talk about data collected from formal and informal assessments, the team determined what kinds of reading strategies would best support Evan. Ryan and Susie would then document Evan's progress as new strategies were implemented, using the Johnson framework that Kristy described earlier.

 Here's What. Evan had participated in Reading Recovery, but those services were discontinued after the maximum twenty weeks of one-on-one support. The literacy team, however, did not feel that Evan was making adequate progress and so decided to provide him with supplemental (Tier 2) small-group reading instruction with Susie.

 So What. Through careful analysis of formal and informal data (including running records, miscue analysis, anecdotal records, observations, and student talk), Kristy, Ryan, and Susie noticed that while Evan was in Reading Recovery, he used two cueing systems—semantics (meaning cues) and grapho-phonemics (visual cues)—to make predictions about words he did not know. However, once Reading Recovery was discontinued, he rarely used meaning and most often used visual cues only. Based on talk about data, the team decided that their goal in both classroom and intervention settings would be to teach for monitoring and cross-checking.

 Now What (in the Classroom). The team decided that the next step for Evan was to work toward using multiple cueing systems, starting with meaning. Since data showed that he tended to rely on only one cueing system when problem-solving, they decided that the "Guess the Covered Word" strategy would help him slow down and think about what he knew. After predicting what would make sense for the covered word, they would ask him to check his prediction with the visual cues. Ryan brought the big book *Case of the Missing Chick* (Frost, 1991) to read with the group; she had strategically covered up a few key words for the children to problem-solve. She began by asking the students to share the strategies they used when they came upon words that they did not know:

> **Evan:** Sound it out.
>
> **Jamel:** You can take away the word.
>
> **Ryan:** Do you mean skip the word, read on, and then come back? Well, that is what I want us to work on today. To skip the word, read to the end of the sentence, and think about what would make sense. In today's story, I have covered words and I want you to try that. Then we will check our guess by seeing if it looks right with the text.

Next, Ryan shared pages from the big book and demonstrated how to cross-check meaning cues with visual cues. She reread the sentence and asked the students to "think about what would make sense."

> **Ryan:** "She took her shopping basket and _____ off to the market."
>
> **Devante:** Went.
>
> **Evan:** Hurried.
>
> **Tyler:** Ran.
>
> **Jamel:** Zoomed.

Ryan reread the sentence with each child's prediction and asked, "Would that make sense?" The children decided that all of their words would make sense. Ryan then said, "Now, let's see which word will work with the text." She uncovered the first letter, *h*. What do you see?" Students then eliminated their guesses by checking it with words that began with an *h*.

> **Ryan:** So can it be *went*? Can it be *ran*? Can it be *zoomed*? Can it be *hurried*? What do you see? Let's check more of the word. h— *u–r*
>
> **Evan:** I was right, it's *hurried*!
>
> **Ryan:** [Reading a second sentence] "'Call me when the chick _____,' she squealed."
>
> **Devante:** Hatches.
>
> **Jamel:** Gets here.
>
> **Evan:** Pops.

> **Ryan:** Let's reread to see if it makes sense. [Rereading each example] These do make sense, but do they match the text? What do you see? [Uncovering the first letter, *a*.] So could it be *hatches*? *gets here*? *pops*? Do they fit?
>
> **Students:** No.
>
> **Ryan:** Let's look through this word.

She began with *a*, then went to *arr* and reread the sentence, including that part of the word. That is when the students predicted *arrived*.

> **Ryan:** What does it mean?
>
> **Evan:** It means *come*.
>
> **Ryan:** So today, when you are reading and you come to a word you don't know, I want you to try this strategy—skip the word and read on to think about what would make sense, then check your guess with the text to see if it matches.

Then What (in the Classroom). Evan successfully used this strategy when prompted to do so. Ryan then planned to look for examples of him applying it independently without her support.

Now What (with the Interventionist). Susie had previously demonstrated the "Guess the Covered Word" strategy with Evan's small group. Next, she focused on providing practice in encountering words students did not know. In this lesson, each child read the text and Susie listened and prompted as needed. As they read, Kristy noticed that Evan said "the" for the word *them*. Evan had monitored his reading and realized something was not right with the meaning when he miscued. He then went back, reread, and self-corrected. When Susie asked him, "How did you know something wasn't right?," Evan said that the sentence didn't make sense. Susie celebrated what Evan did and used his monitoring example as her teaching point.

Then What (with the Interventionist). Susie used the same technique with Evan until he was fluent with this strategy. She worked toward having Evan articulate what he was doing instead of giving him the language to describe his practices. Like Ryan, Susie scaffolded Evan's learning only as needed and helped him strive for independence in cross-checking meaning and visual cues.

Learning through Inquiry and Dialogue: Analyzing Multiple Data Sources and Interpreting through Multiple Perspectives

To support their students' learning, the student literacy team at Ben Hazel Primary School analyzes multiple data sources. Wolcott (2009) argues that analysis follows standard procedures for observing, measuring, and communicating with others about the nature of various kinds of data, and data are examined and reported through procedures generally accepted in schools. Because each assessment procedure has its own limitations and biases, the team analyzes data from a variety of sources, including formal assessments such as the *Dominie* (DeFord, 2004) and informal assessments such as observations, anecdotal records, and running records (Clay, 1993). The focus of these analyses is to create a picture of how a student is learning, and they often result in both quantitative and qualitative descriptions. Assessments function as tools that provide information about a student in a particular moment.

Kristy, Ryan, and Susie, along with members of other literacy teams, go beyond careful analysis of data to interpretation. Interpretation, unlike analysis, is not necessarily derived from agreed-upon, carefully specified procedures, but rather from efforts to make sense of analyzed data (Wolcott, 2009). At Ben Hazel, it goes beyond information gathering to focus on how knowledge informs the kinds of instruction that will support a student. Whereas each person involved in assessment is limited by his or her perspectives on the teaching and learning of reading and writing, interpretation "invites the reflection, the pondering, of data in terms of what people make of them" (Wolcott, 2009, p. 30)—and, as noted in the SARW, "The more consequential the decision, the more important it is to seek diverse perspectives and independent sources of data" (p. 24).

The literacy team accomplishes interpretation through the multiple perspectives brought together through their talk. As literacy coach, it is Kristy's role to create spaces for this kind of interpretive talk. She does this very intentionally. Not only do the team's different perspectives lead to instructional plans for students, but they also allow children like Evan to receive the same instructional focus from multiple teachers. The literacy team creates a common language and common learning experiences for the student.

In the SARW, assessment is defined as a form of inquiry. The end result of any inquiry should be thoughtful new action (Short, Harste, & Burke, 1996). In Evan's case, the team's actions supported his learning. Rather than treating assessment merely as a series of facts about a student, Kristy, Ryan, and Susie took an inquiry stance. Through talk, which they view as the most important way to help them make sense of data and build functional understandings, they built knowledge about both Evan's learning and their teaching. As Kristy noted, "Talk is the breath and life of our process."

While no assessment system is perfect, it is clear that the literacy team at Ben Hazel successfully use multiple perspectives to interpret multiple forms of assessment. They use assessments as tools for inquiry, tools that provide multiple opportunities for the teacher, coach, interventionist, and other educational stakeholders to talk together. In so doing, they learn about their students as readers and about themselves as teachers.

See Figures 17 and 18 for lists of the assessment tools and instructional methods Kristy and Ryan use with their students.

Figure 17. Literacy coach Kristy Wood's assessment tools and instructional moves.

Assessment Tools

Observation

Listening

Inquiry (asking questions to understand)

Johnson's (2006) framework for assessing student learning

Dominie "Oral Reading Passages" and "Sentence Writing and Spelling"

Instructional Moves

Encouraged a cycle of data collection, reflection, and planning between teachers.

Scheduled Student Growth Meetings: Provided time and space for teachers to engage in dialogue as they inquired into and reflected on test data in order to refine teaching practices and better understand student learning.

Reviewed test data with teachers and created environment that allowed teachers to slow down, notice, and name what students were learning.

Brought together vertical and grade-specific teams for analyzing data.

For focus student Evan:

- Provided place to talk about test data as well as informal assessment data from teacher to formulate instruction for Evan.
- Decided that he was not making adequate progress and would benefit from practice with two cueing systems—semantic and grapho-phonemics.
- Determined how or if instruction was working for Evan.
- Aligned Evan's instruction from multiple teachers. Monitored progress with interventionist.

Figure 18. Classroom teacher Ryan Brunson's assessment tools and instructional moves.

Assessment Tools

Listening

Observation

Inquiry (asking questions to understand)

Informal assessments, e.g., over-the-shoulder miscue analysis, running records, anecdotal notes

Dominie "Oral Reading Passages," "Sentence Writing and Spelling," and "Core Reading Words"

Reflection

Instructional Moves

Provided time for students to "turn 'n talk" to each other about their reading as a window into their thinking and to understand the kinds of knowledge they were building.

Determined Evan's abilities with sentence writing and spelling, text reading levels, and core reading words assessment.

Challenged the assumption that Evan did not know high-frequency words and suggested another hypothesis about Evan's reading.

Decided to teach for meaning and cross-checking with text.

Employed "Guess the Covered Word" strategy.

Demonstrated how to read for meaning and cross-checked meaning with text and observed as Evan used these strategies.

Listened to Evan's reading as he cross-checked meaning with text and scaffolded him by rereading, asking questions, and providing practice.

Asked Evan questions about strategies for reading, e.g., "What would make sense here? Which words work with the text?"

Portrait 5: Timothy O'Keefe, Second-Grade Teacher

Heidi Mills and Timothy O'Keefe

Growing a Reader: From Kidwatching to Curriculum

"My Favorite Teacher at CFI"

> My favorite teacher at CFI is Mr. O'Keefe. He has dedicated his own time after
> school for Literacy Club. I actually get excited about the Literacy Club! He really
> cares for ALL of his students. I really like when he plays the guitar in the classroom.
> Thank you, Mr. O'KEEFE, I am actual . . . ly reading now!

This Facebook post was created by Cameron toward the end of her second-grade
year at the Center for Inquiry (CFI) in Columbia, South Carolina. CFI is a suburban magnet school, jointly supported by Richland School District Two and

the University of South Carolina. About 51 percent of the students are European American, 47 percent are African American, and the remaining 3 percent are Korean, Chinese, African, and Latino/a.

At first glance, Cameron's entry is simply adorable, yet it is so much more than simple or adorable. When you look below the surface, her post reveals critical reasons why Cameron closes with this most powerful accolade—she is "actually reading now!" Cameron *is* a reader. Her identity has shifted over the school year. When Cameron entered second grade, she lacked both confidence and competence as a reader. She avoided reading. Now she embraces it. She sees herself as a reader; she is invested in the process. Cameron has a greater sense of agency, and she chooses to read in and outside of school.

At CFI, Cameron was immersed in a culture of literacy, one in which reading was valued and woven throughout the fabric of the curriculum, day in and day out. Cameron's immersion in a culture of literacy at CFI began in kindergarten. Teachers at CFI teach the same group for two consecutive years, so Cameron had 360 days of rich, authentic, meaning-based reading experiences with her kindergarten and first-grade teacher, Jennifer Barnes. Tim, her second-and third-grade teacher, was standing on Jennifer's shoulders as they both made instructional decisions from careful kidwatching data. Both teachers embrace the SARW and believe that "the most productive and powerful assessments for students are likely to be the formative assessments that occur in the daily activities of the classroom" (p. 13). Additionally, Tim collaborated extensively with Cameron's parents. As recommended in the SARW, Tim established an honest, trusting relationship with them and engaged them as valuable partners in the assessment process. He kept Cameron's parents abreast of their daughter's progress by sharing data collected from both formal and informal assessments. In return, they helped Tim understand Cameron's life outside of school. Tim lived the charge laid out to teachers in the SARW:

> Schools have a responsibility to help families and community members understand the assessment process and the range of tools that can be useful in painting a detailed picture of learning, including both how individual students are learning and how the school is doing in its efforts to support learning. (p. 27)

Tim and Cameron's parents worked together to ensure Cameron's success as a reader. They moved in and out of mentor and apprentice roles as they learned about Cameron as a reader and provided her with literacy experiences that propelled her forward.

Why a Culture of Literacy Matters in the Classroom

Classroom teachers can make a significant difference in the current and future life of a child. They have the gift of time—seven hours a day—with their students. When teachers send children ongoing messages about the value and enjoyment found in reading; when they take the time and care necessary to get to know children as readers so they can make wise teaching moves on each child's behalf; and when they teach children how to talk with one another, reader-to-reader, lives change (Mills, O'Keefe, & Jennings, 2004). In Tim's second-grade, self-contained classroom, he uses a variety of curricular structures to help Cameron and her class-mates grow and change as readers, including:

Read-alouds. Reading high-quality picture and chapter books to the class followed by engaging conversations that deepen comprehension and appreciation of the text.

Language appreciation. Shared reading of a poem, article, or song as part of morning meeting rituals. After reading the piece together, the class holds reflective conversations about its meaning and about the author's craft.

Independent reading (IR). Extensive time reading "just right" books independently.

Reading conferences. During IR, Tim coaches his students as readers and audiotapes them as they read passages from their selected books. He also takes notes about fluency, intonation, and the nature of miscues (high or low quality) and concludes each conference by talking about the story, the child's book selection, and the reading strategies used by the student.

Whole-class strategy sharing. Immediately following indepen-dent reading, Tim holds a strategy-sharing meeting for the whole class. He begins the meeting by highlighting the strategies his students used during IR. He then invites them to share the strategies they use to figure out unknown words or passages.

Literature circles. Students regularly participate in small-group conversations around chapter books. They often read a chapter or two for homework, complete a literature response entry, and then come together to talk about the book. The goal is for students to leave the conversation with a deeper understanding and appreciation of the text.

Literacy Club. One afternoon each week after school, Tim meets with a small group of students who need additional, focused support as readers. During these meetings, Tim teaches for strategies. Through ongoing small-group instruction across the year, the majority of these children, all of whom entered the year reading below grade level, end the year reading at or above grade level. Most important, they leave as invested, confident readers who choose to read.

Making Strategic Assessment Choices within and across Literacy Structures

We have learned that it is not enough to simply engage students in rich literacy experiences. Teachers also need to be careful kidwatchers who identify patterns in children's reading and make instructional decisions, using both formal and informal data (Goodman, 1978; Johnston, 2005; Strickland & Strickland, 2000). When doing so, they teach from an inquiry stance (Mills, 2011) and access the potential of each curricular structure. For them, as noted in the SARW, "the most productive and powerful assessments for students are likely to be the formative assessments that occur in the daily activities of the classroom" (p. 13).

When students are engaged in strategy sharing after independent reading, they attend to strategies that accomplished readers use. When they engage in literature circle conversations, the focus is on talking their way into understanding things such as text, plot, and characters. Each curricular structure has different instructional purposes and assessment opportunities. Careful kidwatchers ask questions such as:

- What is the purpose/focus/function of this structure?
- What are the essential questions we want to ask ourselves about children's literacy learning when engaged in this structure?
- What are the natural opportunities to gather information from the process and products that are naturally embedded in the life of this structure?
- How might naturally occurring data help us answer our essential questions about individuals, groups, and our whole class?
- What tool(s) might complement and extend naturally occurring data in this structure to answer our questions and help us make informed instructional decisions and teach responsively (professionally published, teacher-created, created with and for children)?

Teachers need to know about the strategies their students employ, their reading preferences, their investment when given time and choice to read, and the ways in which they respond to texts and to one another. To gather this information, kidwatchers access naturally occurring data within curricular structures and then turn to formal and informal assessment data to fill the voids. They understand that each form of assessment reveals certain things and conceals others. Teachers use assessments rather than being used by them.

Tim has been a classroom teacher for thirty-three years and has become a strategic kidwatcher by creating his own system that is focused yet efficient and captures what he believes matters most as he confers with readers. He documents miscues on sticky notes or on his ELA clipboard, which consists of blank paper divided into sections with each class member's name (see Figures 19). As much as possible, he interprets miscues "in the midst" or immediately following the conference. He codes miscues in this way: NMC (no meaning change), SMC (some meaning change), and MC (meaning change). If students self-correct, he adds SC next to the miscue because he wants to capture the nature and frequency of self-corrections. Just last week, Tim took notes as Cameron, now in third grade, was reading *The Music of Dolphins* (Hesse, 1996). He noticed: "She was focused and ready to read. She read 'if' for *is* and self-corrected the miscue. She read 'probably' for *perhaps* and self-corrected." Tim coded the miscue as NMC because it didn't change the meaning, i.e., it was a semantically acceptable miscue. Cameron sought help for the word *swimmer*. She read "Shay" for *she*, which didn't change the meaning (NMC). Finally, she substituted "waits" for *watches*, which Tim coded as SMC (see Figure 20). He made a note about his teaching point with an asterisk. During this conference, he reminded Cameron about the value of rereading when she miscues because he noticed it has made a difference in her fluency and comprehension over time.

Cameron as a Reader in Second Grade—in Tim's Words

Cameron was absent on Friday. She had missed her student-led conference earlier in the week, and we needed to reschedule. Her brother, Chase, was in school so I asked him about Cameron. "She has a fever," he said. That afternoon, I was pleased to see Cameron in her mom's van as they came to pick up Chase.

"Hi, kiddo. We missed you today," I said reaching into the van to touch her cheek.

"I missed you guys too. I'm feeling better now. Did you read *Holes* (Sachar, 1998) today?" She was referring to the chapter book our student teacher was reading aloud to the class.

"Yes, we read a chapter this afternoon."

"Uh-oh," her mom said. "We read three chapters today."

"Yeah," Cameron said. "We're up to the part where Stanley finds Zero in the desert under the boat. Do you know the part?"

I knew the part. It made me smile to hear that Cameron and her mom had spent a good part of the day reading together. That wasn't always the case for Cameron.

"Sure," I said, "We only read a chapter together, so you're ahead of us."

Figure 19. Tim's kidwatching notes.

Made a personal connection – "My dog can run like
nobody's business", "I like the part that said it was a
race against time – it made me want to read on" enthusiastic
      Garrett

"They put in a lot of cool descriptions about Grandfather
and all the flashbacks so we really get to know
him better... That really makes me care for him."

      Serenity

Wears her glasses today! much better apparent comprehension,
reads a little word-for-word, "It says a lot of details
about how sick Grandfather is. I feel sorry for him."

      Cameron

Talks about his own dog, great personal connection,
"So far I like it because it's about a dog. You know
how much I like dogs!"

      Samuel

" I wonder who the antagonist is who's waiting
on the porch," very invested in the conversation, "How
Little Willie has to feed Grandfather ... I like how we
get to him when he wasn't sick – through flashbacks."
      Brandon

12/5
Reading Stone Fox || Comments in small group/
        whole group

Figure 20. Tim's reading conference notes.

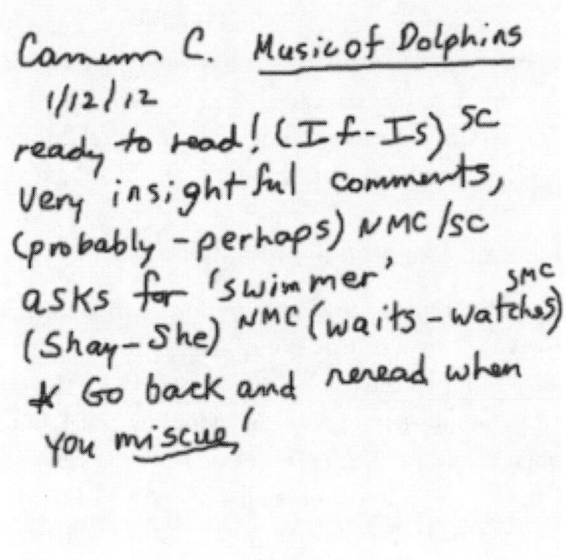

> Cameron C. Music of Dolphins
> 1/12/12
> ready to read! (If-Is) sc
> very insightful comments,
> (probably -perhaps) NMC /sc
> asks for 'swimmer'   smc
> (Shay-She) NMC (waits - watches)
> ✱ Go back and reread when
> you miscue!

"Oh, don't worry," she said. "I won't give it away." And I trusted that she wouldn't. Cameron's mother and I chatted a moment about rescheduling our student-led conference. Chase climbed into the car and before they drove away, I asked Cameron what she would read for her parents at the student-led conference on Monday morning. She beamed. It was a beautiful, confident smile, full of her high dimples and sparkling eyes, one that said so much more than the few words she spoke next: "*Frog and Toad*, of course!"

Now it was my turn to smile. *Frog and Toad Together* (Lobel, 1972). As they drove away into the weekend, I remembered how important Lobel's stories were to Cameron when she was first becoming a reader. When I met Cameron in August of second grade, she avoided reading. I documented a number of instances that revealed this troubling pattern on my clipboard of anecdotal notes. I make ongoing observations of each student, documenting what they say or do during whole-group, small-group, and individual literacy experiences. These notes are really for my eyes only. They are brief yet detailed enough to remind me what mattered at that moment with each individual child (see Figure 19).

When we engaged in shared reading during language appreciation, Cameron did not join in and actually turned away from the text, which was written on large sheets of construction paper or on the Smart Board. When we sang songs together, she did not look at the song chart to read the lyrics, even though I made my expectation clear and reminded the children to do this for the first few weeks of school. When Cameron's peers were discussing a particular passage in small-group literature circle conversations, she did not try to find the relevant page or track down the passage. When one of her friends chose a passage to read aloud, Cameron did not focus on the text enough to even read along. The first time I asked her to read, she was very reluctant. "Couldn't you read with someone else today?" she pleaded. Now Cameron asks if she can read first.

Seeking to Understand Cameron as a Reader

In my initial reading conference with Cameron during the first week of second grade, I asked her to read the first story out of the 2.1 basal reader. I do this with every child at the beginning of the year to give me a feel for the range of readers I have in class. I rarely use the basal texts for reading material, but I do use them for purposes like this and when I need multiple copies of a story for a small- or large-group literature conversation. This year the first text I used to get a sense of readers in the class was *Ronald Morgan Goes to Bat* (Giff, 1990). When I met with Cameron, I took notes as she read softly and hesitantly. I noticed that her energy was devoted to sounding out words, with little regard for meaning. Almost every miscue I recorded reflected visual information or decoding, with little regard for syntax or semantics. She read "hitted" for *heard*, "toaged" for *tagged*, and "team" for *turn*. She frequently pleaded with me to tell her the unknown words.

Cameron offered additional evidence that she was not tracking for meaning or engaging with the text. She did not talk about the story or smile at the funny parts. There was no spontaneous chatter about the characters or the plot. When I asked Cameron to tell me about what she had read, she said that she did not want to talk about it and asked if I could read with someone else. Reading was an unpleasant task for Cameron at the beginning of second grade—something she did to comply but did not enjoy. She was visibly relieved when our conference was over and I told her she could join her classmates in independent reading.

Cameron did not choose to read. During independent reading, I often pause between reading conferences to check on the status of the class—I make notes about book choices and evaluate how invested the students are as readers. My record sheets are simple, triple-spaced rosters, with titles, a few observations, and a rudimentary scoring system, with "scores" ranging from one to three. This simple yet efficient record-keeping strategy helps me learn about my students as readers and reveals important investment patterns. Each time I look to see what a child is doing, I record a "score" on the chart. A "one" signals (as far as I can tell) that the child is reading—his or her eyes are on the text. This is the easy one. A "two" means the student was not reading when I looked his or her way but may have been off-task for just a moment—e.g., had briefly turned away, was looking for a different book, or was enjoying the pictures in the current one. A "three" means that the student is not reading and/or is not consistently engaging with the text. This kind of data is especially important to me at the beginning of the year, as I get to know the children as readers.

To help me identify investment patterns across the class, I try to make at least ten of these observations each week. If the majority of my observations are ones and twos, I feel pretty good about how IR time is being used. If the scores include mostly twos and threes, this tells me that there may be issues that need to be addressed with individual readers or the entire community. It may be that we need to find some "just right" books or perhaps a more suitable reading spot in the room. Or it might just mean that a child is avoiding reading for some reason. Cameron's scores for those first few weeks of school were consistently threes with a few twos. She often chose books that were too challenging for her to read on her own or magazines with text that she couldn't understand. Based on patterns in my independent reading data, one of the first and most important moves I made was to help Cameron learn how to make "just right" book choices. I wanted her to find books she could read successfully so she would find reading enjoyable and employ a range of cue systems to construct meaning, instead of defaulting to "sounding out," which is the pattern I identified during my first conference with her.

I made another critical move when I invited Cameron and four of her classmates to join me for Literacy Club every Thursday after school for about ninety minutes. We begin Literacy Club with fellowship—we straighten up the room, share a snack, and play word games. We then spend at least an hour reading and writing together. If we are reading a book together as a class, we read ahead in Literacy Club. This makes it possible for all of the kids to engage successfully with the texts their friends are reading and allows them to be full-fledged members of what Smith calls the more generalized literacy club (Smith, 1987). Other times, we select a book to read as a small group over a several-week period. We read, talk, share strategies and connections, then read some more. The environment is intimate and nonjudgmental. This close, personal time gives me an opportunity to speak with children reader to reader and friend to friend. Typically, when we reach the end of a page, we talk. We share connections, predictions, and ideas about characters. I share from my notes. I always find something positive to share about each child, and I often coach toward a more holistic, meaning-based set of strategies. As Cameron read in our small group, I provided her with focused feedback, which I subsequently recorded in my kidwatching notes:

> I love how you changed your voice when David was talking, that really shows me
> that you are understanding this page. You can always tell when dialogue is coming up

when you see quotation marks, right? How did you figure that word out? *Mysterious* is a long one. I could tell that you knew it was an exciting part because I could hear it in your voice.

In the beginning, I did all of the coaching in the Literacy Club. Now, all of the children coach and learn from one another. These consistent, weekly literacy engagements have made a tremendous difference in Cameron's confidence and in her competence as a reader. Finding herself in a position to appreciate and coach another student elevated the way she looked at herself as a reader. As the year progressed, she developed a generative theory of reading and used it to coach her friends.

Another essential feature of our classroom that helped Cameron develop as a reader is our emphasis on whole-group strategy sharing. To conclude independent reading, I ask the children to use a sticky note to write down the strategies they use when figuring out unknown words or passages. As they write, they become more aware of the strategies they employ as readers, get in touch with their own reading process, and reflect on their habits or the strategies and patterns they use across texts. I add my own sticky note observations to the mix and access them just as the children do, to remember and highlight effective strategies I noticed individual students using during IR (see Figure 21).

After independent reading, I ask the children to gather at the front of the room for strategy sharing so they can share what they do when they read and how they figure out the meaning of challenging words and passages. At first, Cameron never shared. I think she felt that she had nothing significant to add to the conversation. I continued to nudge her to share every time we conferred. When I read with Cameron in January, I asked if I could share some of what I noticed. Not only did she agree, but she also shyly recorded a strategy of her own, "I look at the pictures." She read what she wrote to the class in a voice barely above a whisper. It was a powerful moment—the very first time she agreed to share in this forum.

"How does looking at the pictures help you figure out what you are reading?" I asked.

"It tells me more about the story," she said, a little breathlessly.

"That's right," I said to the class. "She was sitting next to me, reading a Frog and Toad story, a really cool story, very funny; she turned the page and before she even looked at the words, she told me what she saw in the two pictures. And then she started reading those words. In my notes, I wrote that it helped her to make a prediction about what was going to happen on those two pages. And she was exactly right. Those pictures went with the words so well."

With Cameron's permission, I went on to tell the class some of the things I noticed that might help the other students. I mentioned that Cameron came across

Figure 21. Tim's student and teacher reflections.

the word *skip*. "The sentence read, *skip through the meadow*. First she said 'spit,' then 'skate.' Then she said, 'skip, skip through the meadow.'" Turning to Cameron I asked her, "How did you know that? How did you figure that out?"

"I read along," she said. I then explained that Cameron read the rest of the sentence and then came back to it. Others nodded and agreed with one another that they too used the strategy of reading on and then coming back. This was a breakthrough moment for Cameron. I believe it was transformative. When Cameron changed her mind, she became a reader in her own eyes. She assumed the identity of a reader and took action to help her friends do the same. By contributing to the conversation during strategy sharing, she was assuming a leadership role in the literacy club of our whole classroom.

At CFI we have expanded our vision of kidwatching beyond that of the teacher taking careful notes and then making instructional decisions from kid-watching data (see Figure 22). While we believe that kidwatching begins with the teacher making careful observations and interpretations of children as readers and writers, it doesn't stop there. It becomes even more powerful when children get to know one another as readers and writers and get in touch with themselves and the reading–writing process. Strategy-sharing sessions promote thinking together about the reading process, noticing and naming strategies readers use individually and collectively to construct and share meaning. Strategy-sharing sessions promote all three dimensions of a richer, expanded vision of kidwatching: teachers knowing kids, kids knowing each other and their teachers, and kids knowing themselves as readers, writers, and learners. My classroom does not consist of one teacher and twenty-two learners. We are twenty-three teachers and twenty-three learners.

Figure 22. Expanded vision of kidwatching.

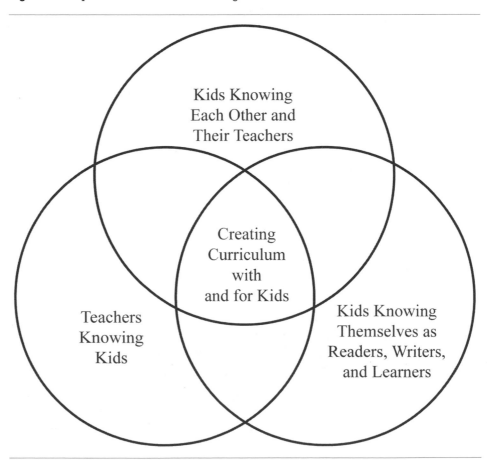

Another positive shift for Cameron came during literature circle conversations, in which she became much more animated about the books we read together. In small-group as well as whole-group conversations, it was obvious that Cameron was investing more and more in the books. "This chapter is one of the best I ever read!" she said enthusiastically toward the climactic end of *Skylark* (MacLachlan, 1994).

In her last two responses to *Caleb's Story* (MacLachlan, 2001), Cameron was so much a part of the story that she responded, "It was intense! When Grandfather tells Caleb that they have to go dig Sarah out of the snow[,] . . . I did not know if Sarah was going to live. . . . I love this chapter. Grandfather stayed!" These comments show she was reading for meaning. She was making predictions. She was understanding and investing in the story line. Cameron loved the story and the reading process. She demonstrated the power of talk as an assessment tool. As noted in the SARW, "[M]uch of the assessment information in classrooms is made available in students' talk about reading and writing" (p. 14).

In March, when we were preparing for student-led conferences, we took several mornings to discuss and reflect on the children's growth and change as readers, writers, mathematicians, scientists, social scientists, and community members. The day the children considered their growth as readers, Cameron responded to the fill-in prompt "This is how I would describe myself as a reader" with "I love it. When it was the first day of school I did not read good but now I am here longer I CAN READ GOOD!! I think I am a good, fast, great reader."

During Cameron's student-led conference, she read one of her favorite stories, "Dragons and Giants" from *Frog and Toad Together* (Lobel, 1972). She read confidently and fluently and with expression. When I asked her to describe why she liked this book so much, Cameron replied, "'Cause I really like the characters. I like how they play together. I like what good friends they are."

Cameron's mother chimed in with, "When I was young, I just loved the story 'Cookies' (Lobel, 1979) about Frog and Toad. When Cameron and I read those, we were just crying and laughing." Then she went on with another milestone for Cameron and one of her "Proud Mom" moments. The previous week, Cameron's brother, Chase, went to a birthday party at a bowling alley. Cameron went along, staying on the sidelines watching. Cameron's mother nearly cried when she said, "And do you know what? Cameron wanted to bring along a book. Can you believe it?"

I *could* believe it. Cameron sees herself as a reader. She truly enjoys reading on her own and delights in sharing information about the stories she reads. As her teacher and her friend, I can't imagine anything more gratifying.

See Figure 23 for a list of assessment tools and instructional methods I use in my classroom.

Figure 23. Classroom teacher Tim O'Keefe's assessment tools and instructional moves.

Assessment Tools

Informal miscue analysis

IR investment checklist

Reading conference notes

Observations during literacy engagements such as language appreciation and singing class songs

Kidwatching notes during reading conferences

Observations made during Literacy Club when students listen to one another read, make notes, and notice and name the strategies their friends are using

Observations made when students reflect on strategies they use to make sense or construct meaning when they come to something (words or passages) they don't understand and then document their strategies on sticky notes

Instructional Moves

Coached explicitly for meaning-based strategies during reading conferences.

Helped Cameron find high-interest, just-right chapter books for Independent Reading.

Invited Cameron to join Literacy Club (90 minutes a week of intensive and meaningful after-school, small-group literacy instruction).

Named and celebrated specific, effective strategies that Cameron used to construct meaning (e.g., use pictures, skip it, ask yourself if it makes sense).

Helped students learn to talk reader to reader and eventually coach one another as readers.

Had students share strategies they used during Independent Reading.

Complemented and extended student reflections by naming strategies used strategically.

Held student-led conferences in which Cameron, her mother, and her teacher all celebrated her growth as a reader by telling stories and offering examples of high-quality miscues, as well as celebrating her capacity to choose just-right books and her investment in reading outside of school.

Third, Fourth, and Fifth Grade

In third, fourth, and fifth grades, the foci from the earlier grades continue: teachers help students develop or solidify a generative theory of reading, as well as the skills and strategies necessary for them to consistently experience success with texts. In addition, teachers at these grade levels help students become explicitly aware of themselves as readers so that they can use that metacognitive knowledge to become increasingly more independent and comprehend more complex texts.

Third grade is often a transition year, as some students enter without a generative theory. The responsibility of the third-grade teacher is to ensure that those students leave not only with a generative theory but also with the necessary skills and strategies to be on the path toward independently comprehending more complex texts. In Portrait 6, district instructional specialist Robin W. Cox visits Sandy Pirkle Anfin's third-grade classroom to document how Sandy accomplishes this by supporting all students as members of a literacy club. Within that club structure, Sandy, like all the teachers in this book, gathers data about her students as readers. She expertly guides the students to notice and name what they do as readers, an extension of the process that Tim detailed for second graders in Portrait 5.

In Portrait 7, university professor Jennifer Wilson and fourth-grade teacher Erika R. Cartledge describe how Erika nudges her students closer to metacognitive awareness by encouraging them to watch themselves while she watches them. Through this lens, she deepens their metacognitive awareness and facilitates personal reflection as a lifelong endeavor. Next, university faculty member Amy Donnelly shows how teacher Amy Oswalt develops systems in her fifth-grade classroom for collecting data that inform her and her students. Amy Oswalt demonstrates how fifth graders can reflect on their own learning and, in turn, become partners with her in evaluating their own progress from the data she collects.

Across all of these portraits, we see affirmation, expert guidance, and self-reflection—the building blocks of independent, strategic readers and writers.

Portrait 6: Sandy Pirkle Anfin, Third-Grade Teacher

Robin W. Cox and Sandy Pirkle Anfin

Growing into the Intellectual Life around Them

Children excitedly enter the room, sharing stories, settling in for the day, and finding books to read. This is my (Sandy's) classroom—a place where I want everyone to feel that it is okay to be where you are. It [the classroom] is a work in progress. By most measures, my students are below grade level. Many are in special education and others receive services from our reading interventionist. Being honest with children about where they are as readers and praising them for their growth is a constant source of tension for me.

I am a third-grade teacher in a Title I school in the suburbs of a mid-size southeastern city. 62% of our students are European American, 36% are African American and 2% are Latino/a. 44% of the children are on free or reduced lunch status. In my five years of teaching, I have come to understand that although I have standards to address, I also have to know my readers and the reading process. I think that the reading process is like building a house. You cannot put a roof on the house if you don't put the walls up first. Reading is the same. You cannot help children achieve standards until they have all the necessary reading processes in place. When I try to help children reach standards without first addressing reading needs, I am wasting my time and theirs. To be an effective teacher, I have to look at what the child knows and is, and is not yet, able to do.

—Sandy Anfin, October 22, 2010

I (Robin) am the elementary language arts instructional specialist in Sandy's district; I have known her for several years. This year I had the opportunity to spend extended time in her classroom and look closely at how she uses assessment data to guide instruction. When I first began observing Sandy, I immediately realized how easily she relates to her students. She is kind, genuinely interested in their lives, and demonstrates understanding in all that she does. It is not uncommon for a child to approach Sandy to tell her about something that happened at home or to mention a concern. Just recently, when a child came to tell Sandy that she had forgotten her report at home, Sandy knelt down and said, "That's okay, you can bring it on Monday." The child's worried look melted away and she returned to her desk with a smile. These small but significant interactions communicate that, to Sandy, teaching is more than knowing or being able to relate content. It is about understanding learners deeply and being concerned about their lives on a personal level. In *Choice Words* (2004), Peter Johnston quotes Vygotsky and adds his own thinking:

> If we have learned anything from Vygotsky (1978), it is that "children grow into the intellectual life around them" (p. 88). That intellectual life is fundamentally social and language has a special place in it. Because the intellectual life is social, it is also relational and emotional. To me, the most humbling part of observing accomplished teachers is seeing the subtle ways in which they build emotionally and relationally healthy learning communities—intellectual environments that produce not mere technical competence, but caring, secure, actively literate human beings. (p. 2)

As part of helping children grow in the intellectual life around them, the stance of kindness that Sandy takes with her students is more than a personality characteristic. It is part of her professional commitment to help all of her students feel that they are special and that they are valued members of the literacy club (Smith, 1987) that Sandy establishes in her classroom. Frank Smith describes the literacy club as a place where readers interact with and learn from one another. As he argued, "We learn from the company we keep" (Smith, 1992, p. 432). Teachers who establish their classrooms as literacy clubs go out of their way to make sure that every child, regardless of ability, sees him- or herself as a successful reader and writer. Sandy accomplishes this by the way she talks with children, by the way she encourages them to talk with one another, by the curricular decisions she makes, and by her efforts to raise their awareness of themselves as readers and writers.

A typical day in Sandy's classroom begins with the third graders gathering on the carpet in front of the easel. Sandy provides a demonstration, usually in the form of an interactive read-aloud, and engages the children in conversations around reading as a meaning-making process. When I spent time in her classroom in September, she was introducing the idea of metacognition: she had co-constructed a chart with the class the day before (see Figure 24). Sandy told the class, "I am going to show you how I am thinking as I am reading. I am going to do some thinking aloud and when I do that, is it a time for you to talk?" The children respond, "No." She then began to read aloud Patricia Polacco's book *Thank you, Mr. Falker* (1998). She stopped a couple of pages into the text and said, "I remember when I was a little girl starting school. I remember wanting to read, so I can understand how the girl in the book feels." This comment is not accidental. Sandy had previously told her students that at one time she did not feel like she was a part of the literacy club: she was not a reader, but now she is and wants them to be also. She continued to read and stopped periodically to demonstrate her own thinking. At the end of the read-aloud, she gave the children time to process this strategy of stopping to think and make meaning. She asked the children why it might be a good idea to do this. One child responded that stopping helps you remember the story and think. Another child said that you can make sure you are understanding the story. Sandy affirmed both children and told the class that today during independent reading she wanted them to try this strategy. She was going to give them sticky notes as a way of marking the places where they stopped, but the most important thing for them to do was to think while they read.

The children then quickly moved from the gathering place on the carpet to their seats, where bags of carefully selected books waited. Sandy noticed a child looking for a book to read and checked in with him to make sure he knew what he needed to do. She then moved to a small table to have a one-on-one conference with another child.

Sandy listened to him read a *Dominie* text (DeFord, 2004) and marked the miscues as he did so. While he finished the book silently, she analyzed the record for meaning and visual cues. When he was done, Sandy asked him to retell the story and followed up with comprehension questions about the book.

As soon as conferences were over and the timer rang, the children returned to the carpet for a debriefing. The talk returned to what they were learning about being strategic readers. Students shared what they tried as readers, what worked and what didn't. They listened intently to one another and often add comments such as "I tried that too!" This is a literacy club in action. Children were talking about books, believing in their ability to make sense of text, and discussing what they were learning about how to stretch themselves. As the district instructional

Figure 24. Sandy's metacognition chart.

Metacognition ⟶

Text + Thinking = Real Reading

Thinking
about our
thinking

Thinking Stems

I'm thinking . . .

I'm noticing . . .

I'm wondering . . .

I'm seeing . . .

I'm feeling . . .

specialist, I see that teachers sometimes skip this opportunity with their students. Sandy understands the value of having children debrief.

When we met to talk about my observations of her classroom, I asked Sandy about her independent reading time. She felt it was critical that students were in love with books and reading ones they could and wanted to read. For this to happen, students needed to first understand that reading was about making meaning. This was often something Sandy needed to help students learn. She noted, for example, that the child she was reading with earlier thought reading was about getting the words right. Other readers were not making inferences, not thinking deeply, while they were reading. She also shared observations of students' use (or not) of picture cues and of monitoring (or not) for meaning. Sandy keeps track of this kind of assessment data and uses it to inform her teaching. She explained her instruction process:

> I think first of all, it's having lots of conversations whole class [about] "What is reading? What does that mean to you?" And kind of fixing some of those misconceptions and . . . helping kids . . . come to the realization of, "Oh, it's not just about if I can say all the words." [In this way, I help] more proficient readers lead some of the less proficient readers to those understandings; [I have] that community talk . . . about books and around what reading is.

And then creating an environment that it's okay to be where you are. . . . I almost cried the other day because I have one child—Nadaria—one of my resource students who refuses to read what's on her level because she's embarrassed about it. And another little boy who is the lowest reader in my class [he's on a 4A], and he heard me talking to Nadaria in the library and she was saying, "But I want to read chapter books." And I was saying, "But Nadaria, if you can't understand the words, then what is the point?" And he leaned over and said, "Nadaria, if you read—the more 'just right' easy books you read—you're gonna get there one day, but we have to read easy books first or we're never gonna get there."

It was clear to me why Sandy almost cried.

In an earlier conversation in the fall, I asked Sandy who had been influential in her learning about reading. She stated, "Well, I think foundationally Frank Smith and that whole idea of the literacy club. I think I always kind of go back to him because I can connect to it, because I didn't feel a part ever until I was in my master's program. And so I think that really shaped [my thinking]. Once I learned about that [the literacy club] and read him that very first class, it was kind of like it made sense why I struggled in school and why I hated school."

As we wrapped up this discussion, I asked Sandy how she made decisions about what to teach each day. She quickly responded that she used her miscue analysis (Goodman, Watson, & Burke, 1987, 2005) on the *Dominie* "Oral Reading Passage" assessment (DeFord, 2004), her anecdotal notes during reading and writing workshops, and her observations during class discussions about reading. She then formed small groups around the patterns she had identified. We continued our conversation, which led to a discussion about her concerns for her student Anton. In first grade, after insistence from his mother that Anton must be learning disabled (his father was, so she thought Anton must be), Anton was identified for special services. As a result, he had an individualized education program (IEP), and he received daily reading instruction from a special education teacher.

At the beginning of the year, Anton had also taken the national Measures of Academic Progress (MAP) test (Northwest Evaluation Association, 2008). He was in the 19th percentile in reading and the 1st percentile in language development. However, while Sandy uses the MAP assessment data as information, she knows that it cannot replace sitting side by side with a child and listening to him read. As noted in the SARW:

> Teacher knowledge cannot be replaced by standardized tests. Any one-shot assessment procedure cannot capture the depth and breadth of information teachers have available to them. Even when a widely used, commercial test is administered, teachers must draw upon the full range of their knowledge about content and individual students to make sense of the limited information such a test provides. (p. 15)

When Sandy first sat with Anton, she interviewed him using the Burke interview (Goodman, Watson, & Burke, 1987) and her own interest inventory. She found that he hated school and specifically hated reading. His interests were in trucks and trains, and he did not want to discuss reading at all. Normally this would not have been a major concern for Sandy, as she frequently encounters children who do not yet love to read. However, because he left the room every day to get help from a special education teacher, Anton spent only fifteen to twenty minutes a day with Sandy for reading. That was not much time for her to help him choose to read.

Sandy was also concerned that the instruction Anton received from the special education teacher might not be consistent with what he received from her. On the *Dominie* "Oral Reading Passage" assessment (DeFord, 2004), Anton's instructional level was an 8A (equivalent to the sixth month of second grade). His meaning cue use was 33 percent and his visual use, 17 percent. He self-corrected at a ratio of 1:7. Sandy's greatest concern was that Anton would not even attempt to read an unknown word. He had few, if any, problem-solving strategies. Sandy wanted to help Anton focus on reading as a meaning-making process. She knew that the focus in the special education classroom would be on sound–symbol relationships.

Sandy subsequently talked to Anton's special education teacher and shared her data. She explained that she thought it was essential for her to match Anton with fun and easy books and that he needed to see reading as an enjoyable experience. It was important to Sandy that Anton develop a theory of himself as a reader and join the literacy club she was establishing in her classroom. The special education teacher agreed to allow Anton to read for meaning and to encourage him to think about what would make sense when he came to words he did not know. She also reduced his special education services time to thirty minutes to allow Anton to be in the classroom for longer periods during reading and writing workshop.

Initially, Anton read slowly; he sounded out every word and had few high-frequency words under control. Sandy started with two goals. First, she wanted to help Anton understand that he was a reader and that reading was a meaning-making process. Second, she wanted him to hear multiple models of fluent reading. She began by matching him with books that were fun and easy for him. When he came to a word he did not know, Sandy gave it to him. She talked to his mother and asked her to do this as well. She also asked Anton's mother to read to him as a way to help him fall in love with books. Sandy gave Anton time with books on an MP3 player and on the computer so he could further experience fluent reading.

Over time, Anton increased his knowledge of sight words and was more confident as a reader. When Sandy saw this shift in him, as evidenced by his willingness to read with her and his desire to listen to books on tape, she decided to start having him "skip the word." Sandy often discussed Anton's progress with him when they met. She wanted him to see that he was growing as a reader and how he was doing this. When she discussed the growth with him, she would often ask him why he thought he was improving. Sandy felt it was important for Anton to take a metacognitive stance, to recognize that these strategies were working and also to understand that his commitment was making a difference.

Skipping words worked well for a while, and because he was reading at appropriate text levels, Anton was able to comprehend much of what he read. In time, Sandy decided that she wanted him to substitute meaningful words when he came to those he did not know. At this point, she hit a block. Anton refused to do it. He started sounding out words again, and even when she covered a word for him, he refused to make substitutions. Sandy decided to stop asking him to do this. She went back to having him skip the word and then, at the end of portions of the text, she would talk to him and ask him what was happening. She found that when she did this, Anton would describe what had happened and his vocabulary matched many of the words he had ineffectively tried to sound out.

Sandy also saw a shift in Anton when he began asking her if he could listen to chapter books on tape. He wanted more sophisticated texts and she made sure he had them. At this time, Anton independently decided to read SpongeBob SquarePants books. Sandy initially underestimated the power of using a text about characters that Anton knew from television. However, she quickly realized that because Anton could "hear" the voices and knew the actions, the books were easier for him, and he was able to read the SpongeBob SquarePants books fluently. To Sandy's delight, Anton also independently began making meaningful substitutions for unfamiliar words.

On a *Dominie* (DeFord, 2004) text reading in March, Anton read a *Dominie* 10A (seventh month of third grade) text with 100 percent comprehension and 95 percent accuracy. He had gained nine months over the course of seven. Anton's fluency still needed work, but he had improved considerably since the fall. The biggest change Sandy saw was that he was choosing to read, and he used more effective strategies to figure out unfamiliar words. On the Measures of Academic Performance (Northwest Evaluation Association, 2008), Anton was in the 72nd percentile in reading (compared to 19th percentile in the fall) and the 26th percentile in language development (compared to the 1st percentile in the fall).

Sandy hoped to have Anton more secure in his strategy use by year's end. His use of meaning cues was still around 20 percent; Sandy felt it would take a bit more time for him to learn to use both meaning and visual cues. However, he was attempting unknown words, he had developed a desire to read, and he had grown in his ability to make sense of text.

Sandy is committed to every student in her classroom and knows that the most powerful information is the assessment data that provide explicit direction for instruction. As stated in the SARW:

> A teacher who knows a great deal about the range of techniques readers and writers use will be able to provide students and other audiences with specific, focused feedback about learning. Indeed, students learn things about themselves and about literacy from teachers' feedback that no standardized test can supply. (p. 15)

Recently, Sandy held another conference with Anton to discuss his progress and share her excitement at his reading and effort. She asked him what he thought he had done to improve and was pleased when he said that, originally, when he didn't know a word, he skipped it, and now he went back to reread and think about the book. He said he was happy about his growth as a reader. He had become more aware of himself as a reader and was seeing himself as a part of the literacy club.

See Figure 25 for a list of assessment tools and instructional methods Sandy uses in her classroom.

Figure 25. Classroom teacher Sandy Anfin's assessment tools and instructional moves.

Assessment Tools

Listening

Observation

Inquiry (asking questions to understand)

Anecdotal notes

Burke interview

Modified miscue analysis

Dominie "Oral Reading Passages"

Measures of Academic Progress (MAP)

Instructional Moves

Helped students find books that are both fun and easy.

Helped students develop a sense of agency.

Provided books on tape to help develop fluency.

Demonstrated fluent reading through read-alouds and shared reading.

Allowed use of texts such as SpongeBob books.

Focused on meaning for prompts during independent conferences and also during whole-class and small-group lessons.

Ensured that all remarks help students develop agency.

Provided time for students to engage in reading and writing.

Portrait 7: Erika R. Cartledge, Fourth-Grade Teacher

Jennifer L. Wilson and Erika R. Cartledge

"They Always Know My Eyes Are on Them": Using Kidwatching to Inform Teaching

Erika's Classroom

Erika Cartledge's fourth-grade classroom is truly a community of learners, one in which students have frequent opportunities to express themselves and make informed choices. It is a print-rich environment with a well-organized, attractive, and easily accessible classroom library. Anchor charts surround the room. A meeting area is set up at the front of the room. Students sit at tables, which are grouped heterogeneously. A kidney table located in the left front corner is used for conferences, small-group instruction, and assessments. The twenty-one students in Erika's classroom are racially, educationally, and economically diverse—52.0 percent are African American, 29.0 percent are European American, 9.5 percent are Latino/a, and 9.5 percent are Asian American. Two of the students have an IEP or 504 plan, and 38 percent qualify for free or reduced lunch.

A Typical Day

On a typical day, the students enter the classroom when the first bell rings at 7:40. They follow the morning routine, which includes reading the interactive morning message and listening to the morning announcements. Around 8:05, the class musician plays a CD of "Colorful World," a transitional song for reporting to the meeting area for morning meeting. Then the students greet one another and hold share time. Two students sign up each day to share something about what the class is learning, what they as a community have learned, or what they will be learning. Erika uses this time to learn about and from her students.

The Helper of the Day then reads the interactive morning message. In this classroom, the students are in charge—they practically run the classroom. The students take the lunch count, set up the technology, facilitate morning meeting, and more. When discussing these tasks and the students' responsibility for them, Erika emphasizes the importance of trust: "Trust is a huge factor. In order for everything to work well, I have to trust myself, the students, and the process."

During morning meeting, Erika launches reading workshop, which includes high-quality read-alouds, shared reading, and word study within a content workshop. Independent reading and writing take place daily for thirty minutes each after related arts. Math workshop follows writing workshop. After lunch and recess, the class conducts further exploration of content literacy. To support the learning of US history, Erika uses readers theater, book clubs, content clubs, poetry, and songs. The day of learning concludes with hands-on science exploration.

One day during reading workshop, I captured this reading conference:

Erika: Nicole, what will you be reading today?

Nicole: *Judy Moody* [McDonald, 2000].

Erika: Okay, *Judy Moody*. . . . What made you check out that book?

Nicole: Because in the summer I read . . . I read the first book *Judy Moody* and I thought it was really good, so I'm reading the second one.

Erika: Okay . . . wonderful . . . and how many books are in this series? Do you know?

Nicole: Six.

Erika: Six books . . . okay . . . so I'm thinking you have plans to keep going.

Nicole: Yes, ma'am.

Erika: Yes, okay . . . so where are you in this book? And I will need you to speak up please, ma'am.

Nicole: Yes, ma'am . . . I'm at the beginning of the book.

Erika: Okay.

Nicole: And so far Judy Moody wants to be famous because her friend . . . ummmm . . . Jessica Finch got famous about the spelling bee, and she wants to look up words to spell.

Erika: All right . . . I'm going to get you to pick up where you left off on page 26, I guess.

Nicole: Yes, ma'am.

Erika: All right, and remember, I do need you to speak up.

Nicole: Yes, ma'am.

[Nicole reads page 26 and part of page 27.]

Erika: All right, stop right there, please. Thank you very much. Do you think this is a "just right" book for you, Nicole?

Nicole: I think it's kind of easy.

Erika: Yeah, it seems to me too like it's easy. I know you're enjoying it . . . right? And it's almost like you know all the words or almost all the words. Okay . . . and sometimes it's okay for us to read easier books as long as we make sure in our diet that we have some that are going to stretch us a little bit more as a reader.

Nicole: Yes, ma'am.

Erika: Okay . . . all right . . . thank you very much.

Nicole: You're welcome.

Getting to Know Her Students

Erika conducted this particular conference at the beginning of the school year as part of her "getting to know" each reader time. From her observations, interactions, and a reading–writing survey, she had already learned that Nicole read and wrote independently and with a purpose, had a balanced reading diet, liked to read mysteries, made connections when she was reading, used expression, read on grade level, and thought that to be a good reader "[y]ou have to read different books and genres." Erika knew that Nicole thought reading was easy for her when "it's all quiet" and hard when "there's a lot going on." She also knew that one of Nicole's goals was "to read more science books," and that the best books she had ever read were Ron Roy's A to Z Mysteries.

Erika asks students to choose the book to share in these reading conferences; as she noted, "I have no way of knowing which book they will choose. . . . Book selections reveal so much about them as readers. I get a small window into a reader's favorite genre, book series, overall interests, and their level of confidence as a reader." During the book conference, Erika pays close attention to what the students are reading. She considers it both her responsibility and the students' to "monitor their reading diets." Erika believes that reading in just one genre will not help students grow as readers. At the same time, she "make[s] every effort to support their favorite genre." To do this, Erika makes sure to give her students plenty of time and space for book talks. She feels that this empowers them as readers.

As Erika listened to Nicole read, she noted that Nicole read for meaning and self-corrected when meaning broke down. She made one miscue that was not self-corrected ("carton"/*cartoon*) and two that were corrected ("even"/*everybody* and "we were"/*were*). Nicole's pacing and use of expression was appropriate and she attended to punctuation. On other days and in other conferences, Erika used retrospective miscue:

> This type of reading conference [retrospective miscue] allows me to share my noticings on the running record with the reader on the spot. Questions I have about this reader could possibly be answered during this time. I certainly become more knowledgeable about this reader and his or her reading process.

While Erika conducts reading conferences in the classroom or works with small groups, the other students read independently. Sometimes this independent time involves readers theater and book clubs. Students maintain a reader's notebook that includes a monthly reading diet graph, twice-weekly written responses, and an accountability log. Erika explains:

> It's important for my readers to see themselves as readers. We begin the year talking about what readers do and how they can live a reading life. The reader's notebook is simply a system for kids to be accountable for their reading. Each day, my readers record the date, title, pages read, and how they felt about themselves as a reader. They only respond in writing to their reading twice a week. The accountability log reveals to me book completion or abandonment, the way a reader feels about how he or she spent his or her reading time, and communication of the genre. Is this reader choosing "just right" books? Is this reader stuck in a genre or series? The written responses uncover strategies that this reader could possibly be using such as finding places in the text that are confusing, visualizing, questioning the text, making predictions or inferences, etc.

Involving Parents

In the student conference described earlier, Erika asked Nicole a couple of times to speak up so she could be heard clearly on the recordings that Erika shares with parents. In her conferences with them, Erika gives parents a copy of their child's text so they can follow along and encourages them to write on the sheet and share their observations with her about their child. Erika has found that sharing these recordings with parents helps position the parents as their child's advocate and first teacher. This allows parents to see firsthand why, for example, "sounding it out" is not the only possible reading strategy. Indeed, Erika intentionally makes a point of having parents prompt more for meaning: Does that make sense? What would make sense? Erika encourages parents to give her feedback about the conversations she and they have: What was most beneficial? What suggestions do they have? Erika has found that most parents love hearing their child's voice while seeing what their child is doing as a reader, and she plans to continue engaging parents in these authentic conversations. The parents' feedback helps inform Erika's instruction, and she hopes that the language she models to support readers will become a part of the students' home language. These conferences also help parents understand just how well Erika knows their child as a reader, writer, and learner. What a valuable strategy for teaching parents how to have an authentic literacy conversation! Erika shares more about this process:

> When the parents first arrive, I provide them with a note-taking sheet that basically outlines our agenda. I share celebrations first and then summarize their child's reading life. This year, I began this portion of the conference with a video of their child performing a readers theater performance of autumn poetry.
>
> Then I move into reading survey results. Parents get to "see" my thinking based on informal data/direct quotes I have taken from their child. It brings me joy to see the parents' faces "light up" when they hear their child articulate strategies and reveal their reading confidence. My favorite part of the conference comes next. I tell parents, "We will now listen to a voice recording of your child reading. Here is the text that your child chose to share with us at this conference. Please feel free to mark on the sheet. We will discuss our reader after the text is read." We then talk reader to reader, not just teacher to parent, about what we notice. I ask parents, "Is this consistent with what you are noticing at home?" This allows me to position the parents as an advocate for their child and to show the true meaning of a team: the child, parent, and teacher. Parents often say things like "This is what I see at home"; "He sometimes leaves out words when he reads"; "She reads fast like me"; "I would like her to read more like she's speaking"; "I want him to read for understanding because it's essential"; "She has been wanting to read more independently"; "Her reading is a lot better than last year"; "He doesn't like to read. I've tried everything"; "He used to love to read but lost interest in it last year." Last, we then talk about the child's reading diet: How balanced is this reader's diet? How do I begin helping this reader choose other genres to read?

Kidwatching

Erika's smooth, intentional orchestration of her reading and writing workshops is grounded in her *kidwatching* abilities. Kidwatching, first coined by Yetta Goodman in 1978 and then extended by Dorothy Watson in 1992, is a staple in an effective classroom. Kidwatching gives teachers insight into their students' literacy learning through:

- Intensely observing and documenting what students know and can do,
- Documenting their ways of constructing and expressing knowledge, and
- Planning curriculum and instruction that are tailored to individual strengths and needs (Owocki & Goodman, 2002).

Teachers who are strong kidwatchers rely on their theoretical knowledge of reading and the personal and sociocultural factors that influence children's literacy learning. Kidwatchers document their observations through field notes, anecdotal notes and checklists. However, they don't stop at observation and documentation. Effective kidwatchers use the data they collect to make instructional decisions. The International Reading Association and the National Council of Teachers of English (IRA–NCTE, 2010) emphasize the importance of this process in *Standards for the Assessment of Reading and Writing* (SARW), particularly Standard 2, in which they posit that the teacher is the "primary agent" (p. 13) of assessment information and should not be a passive consumer of the data:

> Because of such important consequences, teachers must be aware of and deliberate about their roles as assessors. . . .
>
> [A]s agents of assessment, teachers must take responsibility for making and sharing judgments about students' achievements and progress. (pp. 13–14)

As teachers engage in kidwatching, they are actively observing students, collecting data, and making informed classroom decisions. The agentive role that teachers take on as kidwatchers expands the traditional view of assessment and creates a more responsive and flexible approach to informal assessment. Consistent with the SARW, "[M]uch of the assessment information in classrooms is made available in students' talk about their reading and writing" (p. 14).

Beliefs about Teaching and Learning: "I Had to Get My Beliefs and My Practice Realigned"

Erika taught for twelve years and then left the classroom for four years to work as a literacy coach. The year before she became a coach, she was a partner-teacher with the district literacy coach. She was able to see firsthand how best practices in literacy produced lifelong readers and writers. Through exploration of these practices and ongoing collaboration, Erika became more knowledgeable about reading process, research, theory, and best practices, and, from her perspective, she also became a much better teacher of readers. This reflective practice allowed her to continually examine her beliefs in relation to practice. She asked herself, "What are my beliefs? What are my current practices? If I believe that learning is social, then how am I providing space and time for my students to talk?"

During and after her year as a partner-teacher, Erika participated in a four-year, intense professional development sequence that included study groups of teachers and administrators. This ongoing network was truly life changing for her. The first year allowed her to focus on her classroom instruction, and the following year she moved into a literacy coaching position. Recently, she returned to the classroom. As she explained to me:

> This is me. I had to get my beliefs and my practice realigned. I needed to be grounded in some real theory. I needed to be able to say, "My room is set up like this because learning is social. Why do I have an interactive word wall? Because learning is playful." If you ask, I can tell you why, rather than just saying, "because they told me to" or "because everyone else is doing it."

Erika's strong theoretical background in sociocultural literacy learning means that she sees learning as social (Vygotsky, 1978) and that she creates opportunities for students to talk and interact in small and large groups. She also understands that learning is playful, and she creates an environment in which students can enjoy language. She believes that instruction should be authentic and so creates literacy engagements that encourage students to position themselves as real readers and writers. She sees both students *and* teachers as learners and experts (Short, Harste, & Burke, 1996) and encourages students to share what they are learning with one another. Last, she believes that effective literacy instruction offers students choice and allows for voice and ownership (Johnston, 2004).

Combining these beliefs, Erika implements a balanced literacy approach that creates a predictable structure in her class. At the beginning of the year, she works with her students to create procedures and routines through shared writing pieces. First, the students decide what the morning and dismissal routines will be. Once they agree on a draft, Erika publishes it by posting it in the classroom. The students also decide what their expectations should be during independent reading and writing times. They call this "Our Workshop Guidelines." During this time, while simultaneously getting to know them as readers and writers, Erika creates opportunities to help the children choose books, chats with them about what they like and dislike, and teaches into the data that surround her:

> You need to get to know your kids. I use the first two to three weeks of school just getting to know them. You wouldn't believe how much information I have gained just from that. That intimate setting in the beginning, one on one, you have to start there. I don't make assumptions. I model what conversation should look and sound like. When I launch something—I don't launch too many things at one time—we talk about "What is it? What should we expect to see? What should we expect to do?" I

get a lot of feedback in here from them. Once we generate our own guidelines, then I am looking and listening for what we have decided as a class or set as expectations. We come to a compromise.

Erika draws extensively on one-on-one reading and writing conferences with her students:

> Before when I used to have a student conference, it was very stressful. Once I made the shift and saw conferences as a conversation between readers, it took away a lot of stress. Letting the students lead by asking, "How's it going?" Asking a little question like that you get so much information! I find out answers to questions like these:
>
> - Does this child see himself as a reader?
> - What kind of environment does this reader prefer?
> - Does this child understand what reading is?
> - Does the reader have other strategies besides "sounding it out"?
> - Is this reader able to set a reading goal?
>
> Learning to talk reader to reader did not evolve overnight for me. Not until I treated this special time as a conversation did I realize the joy of conferring. When the teacher places him- or herself in the position of a reader and not as the all-knowing teacher, then space is there to become a learner and not the only expert. I no longer have to be the mind reader. My language now sounds like: "What did you think about your reading just now? I noticed that you were using your finger. What does this do for you as a reader? Is it working well for you?"

Erika intentionally plants the seeds of learning in her classroom environment and instruction and then lets her students grow as readers. She explains:

> If you are not actively engaged in the classroom, you aren't going to get that from the students. Readers don't waste their time. When you plant the seed that learning is important, they are going to really take ownership of it.

Eitelgeorge, Wilson, and Kent (2007) state that "[r]eading and writing are complex processes that call for multiple layers of assessment" (p. 52). Erika agrees with this; she understands that literacy is more than word calling or answering basic comprehension questions. She observes while her students engage in literate interactions. These kinds of observations allow her to more closely align her instruction with what she knows is important for the growth of her students. Erika explains that this was a significant shift for her. In the past, she considered the classroom "hers." Now she makes deliberate efforts to give the students a voice. In the past, she felt she was teaching subjects, not students. Now she teaches students, and her role looks more like that of a teacher-facilitator. Because she better understands the conditions that support learners, she provides more time for reading and writing and focuses more on what students are doing. During book clubs, she listens to the language her readers are using. "Do they know how to talk as readers? Is it appropriate talk? Does it sound artificial? Are they really talking reader to reader? Who is participating? Who is not?" During readers theater practice, Erika looks closely and listens carefully for the ways students support one another as readers: "No, the author wanted it read this way" versus "You keep reading it wrong," or "Please show more expression" versus "That's not how you read a question!" Erika believes that she should hear students using with one another the language she uses with them: "If there is not, then maybe I am not using it as consistently as I had thought."

Organizing for Kidwatching

Erika is an extremely knowledgeable and organized teacher. When she is observing students, she knows what she is looking for and she keeps track of her documentation in a systematic way. Her students know that she is always watching them: "They always know my eyes are on them." Kidwatching takes place every day. Erika constantly shares with the students what she notices: e.g., "I saw you doing that and I want to know more about it." The students know that Erika is going to ask them questions like "What kind of a reader were you today? What kind of a writer were you today?" Erika often compares her notes and observations with how the students answer such questions and develops her lessons around areas where her notes and the students' responses do not match. Sometimes, for example, she reteaches theme or spends more time helping students understand point of view. Erika explains:

> Anecdotal notes for me are informal data that inform my instruction. If we are in independent reading, I'm looking to see if they are using a particular strategy. I am looking at the level of engagement. "Are they enjoying the text they are reading and being strategic about their reading?" It reminds me of what my next teaching point will be, the next conversation with readers and writers. It is a way for me to have a focused conversation. I also like to know what my children are noticing.

Erika also encourages the children to share what they are learning about themselves. She does this because she believes that students need to share their learning among themselves and see themselves as experts:

> We have a strategy share in case I didn't see something. It's important that children can articulate the moves they are making. There are two designated opportunities for students to share. One is during morning meeting following the greeting. The second is strategy share, which occurs at the end of independent reading and writing. This basically involves me posing the question: "What move or moves did you make as a reader or writer today? Who would like to share something that he or she did that

made a difference in their reading today?" I ask the children to make their thinking and/or new learning public.

During this share time, students make these kinds of comments: "When I was reading this chapter book, I was confused about who was saying what, so I . . .";
"While I was reading this nonfiction book, I did not know how to pronounce this word, and so I read ahead and thought about what would make sense"; "I wanted to find out how Ferdinand Magellan died, so I used the index in my book"; "I made a prediction and found out on page _ that I was right"; "I know that I inferred on this part of my book because . . ."; "I know that this book is a myth because . . ."
Erika comments on this:

> The students' sharing supports what we are doing in the classroom. I am in learner mode and I absolutely love it. This is definitely the gradual release of responsibility [Pearson & Gallagher, 1983]. I am taking it back to the kids. They do such a wonderful job of going to the text on their own and sharing pieces of information that helps us all see that strategy in a new way. It is certainly a celebration for us as learners.

Kidwatching has become natural to Erika. She does it without even recognizing she is. It is a part of how she sees her role as a teacher. She is continually observing what students are doing, comparing it to what she knows literacy learners need, and making adjustments to her instruction from that data:

> During independent reading, I am looking to see if students are pretending to read. I watch for facial expressions, conduct quick conferences (e.g., "Tell me about what you are reading" or "What are you reading right now?") and pay attention to whether their reading diet is balanced. I look at their reader's notebook—they keep a reading graph of genres—and sometimes I have to say, "Sweetheart, I'd like to see you add more of ____ to your reading diet." In thirty minutes, I can confer with my whole class.
>
> Shared reading takes place every single day, and it is a strategic teaching time for me to recognize what the students are doing. Even when it is whole group, I can make those notes. I am on the spot. If I am noticing it, I can take action so that the misconceptions don't continue.
>
> I look for celebrations, things that might be challenges, things I need to reteach. I think "this is not working" or "they totally misunderstood what I was asking them to do" or "they are not owning this." Kidwatching is so important because if you put the time in up front, they will eventually own their learning. Book clubs—they own it. Author's chair—they own it. I am just very direct. We don't play games with their learning—i.e., "I noticed that you made three trips to the classroom library; now you only have twenty minutes left—why?" For the most part, they want to be a reader who uses his or her time wisely. The conversations are open and transparent with the kids so all members of the community are clear about what each other is thinking, wanting, expecting, and showing.

When Erika first began systematically collecting data through kidwatching, she tried several different formats to help her organize the information. However, as kidwatching became more natural, she eventually "grew out of forms." In the past, she used a binder with individual sheets to record notes for each reader and writer. Other times she had a checklist attached to a clipboard, a daily "Kidwatching Report," which she compiled in a binder, and then she used grids in a lesson plan book to record data. She no longer tries to keep all her data in one place:

> I'm still taking notes, but it's not all in one place. If it's formal data, like a running record, then I write my notes on the actual piece of data. The look is more conversational. There are more sticky notes and class spreadsheets. I know my readers better. Little notes here and there like "Continue to work on ___" or "Still needs to read through the end of words" or "Phrasing is excellent."

Erika often synthesizes data across students (see Figure 26), allowing her to see her entire class at a glance. This was a whole new way of teaching for Erika. At first she was uncomfortable taking the time to write her anecdotal notes, but she soon learned the value of documenting her kidwatching:

> I am not a sitting teacher. But I've had to make myself sit an extra two minutes to keep up with the paperwork. Every minute counts for me if I am going to maximize my instructional time. I say, "Erika, give yourself those two minutes. It's okay!" Those two minutes allow me to think more deeply while analyzing my data. Does the reader have a sense of story? Can the reader retell? What percentage of miscues have meaning? Is this reader reading at the word level? What reading behaviors did I observe (asking for assistance, using finger to track text, failing to honor punctuation, not reading through the end of words)? Which cueing systems does the reader have under control? Is there a balance of cueing systems used? Is this reader self-monitoring for meaning? What could it be that this reader is or is not doing?

Johnston (1997) reminds us that "viewing assessment only as a set of techniques for collecting data will not get us very far" (p. 157). Erika, however, not only has techniques, but she also knows what she's looking for and she gives herself time to record what she notices. This grounds her instruction.

Using Data to Inform Instruction

Erika explains that her kidwatching and subsequent anecdotal notes let her "go deep rather than broad" with her teaching and allow her to focus her instruction on the specific needs of her students:

> Kidwatching helps me to see the needs (individually, small group, and whole group). I know what needs to be taught and how to best teach into this need. It clarifies the best balanced literacy structure to use. It also lets me know how well the scaffolding/

Figure 26. Sample of Erika's synthesis across students.

	AUGUST	Focus on...
Low Meaning and High Visual	Monet (11) Raymond (11) Precious (11) Jamie (11)	Meaning
High Meaning and Low Visual	NONE	Meaning
Low Meaning and Low Visual	Jason (7B) Christian (11) Jared (10) Kentrell (10)	Nicole (11) Cedric (11) Grace (11) Chad (11) David (11)
	Diane (10) Craig (11) Brigette (10B)	Meaning
High Meaning and High Visual	NONE	

gradual release process is going. Is more or less teacher support needed? Do the learners own the process?

Erika often shares her anecdotal notes with her students:

> I share this kidwatching report with the children. They need to know what my observations are as well. How are things really going? I first begin to look at the "Celebrations," which helps to confirm that specific learning has occurred and/or provides

evidence of prior mini-lessons taught. Am I seeing evidence of my teaching? The "Challenges" lead to additional mini-lessons (management, content, strategy). Where do we need to move from here?

Consistent with the IRA–NCTE *Standards for the English Language Arts* (1996), Erika wants her students "to participate as knowledgeable, reflective, creative, and critical members of a variety of literacy communities" (p. 3). At times, this is a collaborative effort:

> There are always opportunities for kids to give feedback. How did book clubs go today? Let's give this writer or group "a plus, a wonder, and a wish." In the beginning, I have to give them prompts as I teach how the language should sound: A plus would be something like "I like the way you . . ." A question might be "I wonder how/what/ why . . ." A wish could be "Please next time . . ."

By taking what she notices and directly turning that into instruction, Erika "maximizes her instructional time." This allows her to be more intentional in her teaching: "Kidwatching has certainly made me a more reflective teacher-learner. Because of it, I tend to make fewer assumptions but more informed decisions. What really matters now? What could really be going on?" This intentional-ity is what the SARW refer to as the teacher being the primary agent rather than the passive consumer of assessment data (p. 13). Erika is not a slave to the data; instead, she uses data as one more tool to meet her students' needs. As articulated in Standard 2 of the SARW: "The sense [teachers] make of a student's reading or writing is communicated to the student through spoken or written comments and translated into instructional decisions in the classroom" (p. 13).

Pulling It All Together

Erika's curriculum is grounded in her kidwatching. She explains that, through her kidwatching, she is more able to "identify patterns, such as gaps/misconcep-tions, 'ah-ha' moments, wonderings, etc." Kidwatching, for Erika, reveals what her students are "using but confusing," which is what she sees as their instructional level. She sees herself as a teacher of readers and writers, as opposed to a teacher of reading and writing:

> When I "taught reading and writing," I missed the naturally occurring data right before my eyes. I did not know what to look or listen for. I used to be the basal queen while teaching programs. The textbook writers were making decisions for my students that I should have been making. Ultimately, it takes you getting in touch with your own reading process before you can begin to understand that of your students.

This switch in her perspective helps her feel more connected to the needs of her learners. She credits this connection to her kidwatching abilities. She explains: "My students know that their learning matters to me and that learning is not an option—it's required—when we are together in our class community. My eyes and ears are always open for looking and listening." Consistent with Standard 11 of the SARW, Erika explains that she and her students "are there for one another, benefiting from one another's insights and knowledge."

Teaching in this way requires a strong understanding of what readers and writers need to be effective, and that requires a teacher who is willing to take the time to observe closely, document clearly, and create instruction with intentionality. Erika describes this process best:

> Data is everywhere! It is naturally occurring in the classroom. We just need to take time to see it, take time to listen to it. The sticky notes that students use during independent reading—they tell me what this child thinks. This is data. It's everywhere. It tells me so much. It tells me where they are in their thinking. I learn so much about each student and the class as a whole from the conversations that go on throughout the day. I know that data is everywhere! If we make the time for it, it can be an amazing thing for our instructional decisions.

See Figure 27 for a list of the assessment tools and instructional methods Erika uses in her classroom.

Figure 27. Classroom teacher Erika Cartledge's assessment tools and instructional moves.

Assessment Tools

Listening

Observation

Inquiry (asking questions to understand)

Anecdotal notes

Anchor charts of kids' responses

Notebooking

Exit slips

Student reflection

Modified miscue analysis

Dominie "Sentence Writing and Spelling" and "Oral Reading Passages"

Words Their Way spelling inventory

MAP and PASS testing

Instructional Moves

Conducted morning meeting to launch literacy and content workshops.

Used Smart Board and document camera for shared reading.

Focused on reading as meaning.

Provided daily time for independent reading and writing.

Encouraged readers theater.

Established book clubs.

Used flexible, small-group instruction.

Had students share strategies.

Used an author's chair.

Developed interactive morning messages.

Provided talk time.

Created a literacy-rich environment.

Portrait 8: Amy Oswalt, Fifth-Grade Teacher

Amy Donnelly and Amy Oswalt

Finding Children's Strengths: Assessment as a Thinking Process

Amy Oswalt teaches fifth graders in an emerging suburban neighborhood near a southern metropolitan city with a population of more than 100,000. The school serves 815 children, 97 percent of whom are European American and 4 percent of whom are African American, American Indian, Asian, or Latino/a. Of the twenty-two students in her classroom, twenty are European American, one is Latino/a, and one is African American. In her classroom, Amy develops systems for collecting data that inform her instruction (whole group, small group, and one on one) and that are self-informing for students and parents.

Amy develops her vision for this system before ever meeting the children. She modifies this plan throughout the school year—and makes it meaningful—as she gets to know the children as readers, writers, and social scientists. She explains:

> Reading and writing are complex processes. Knowing children well is the key to mak-
> ing standards work to facilitate learning. The state standards are great guidelines, but

they are not a step-by-step checklist to be followed. To teach and assess using standards as the ultimate checklist would result in the curriculum becoming meaningless
to students. When planning for our year, the fifth-grade teachers at my school work
hard to try to unite the reading and writing standards. We draft units of study that
help children learn standards through the real acts of reading or writing. This is one
way we initially try to keep instruction and assessment authentic. This also helps keep
learning flowing. What we want to avoid is choppy instruction that happens when
teachers address one standard or one skill at a time. This means that we look at the
standards and make decisions on which reading and writing standards could be best
addressed within the same units of study.

Let me break that down. We usually start with the writing standards and see
which genres of writing students are expected to learn. We then look at reading
standards while intentionally keeping our final writing product for the unit of study
in mind. For example, when we designed our nonfiction unit, we began with the
nonfiction writing standards. We created a rubric that incorporated them. Then we
looked at the reading nonfiction standards. We designed lessons that incorporated the
nonfiction standards smoothly into our everyday study of nonfiction. We then added
some of those concepts into our rubric. We all actually began the nonfiction unit with
reading. That way, children are able to learn about nonfiction by reading nonfiction.
Over time, children become comfortable talking about the genre and the text features
commonly used. After a couple weeks of immersing ourselves in nonfiction, we took a
look at the nonfiction rubric and began our writing.

This is the way we begin thinking and planning our yearlong instruction. This
kind of planning helps me have learning destinations firmly in mind as the year begins
and helps me feel more comfortable in letting the children's strengths and needs
guide my daily instruction and keep learning purposeful.

Amy's initial system for assessing and evaluating young readers and writers intentionally integrates both standards and thinking with colleagues; put into
practice, this approach helps children see and understand the interplay between
authentic acts of reading and writing. By focusing data collection on the processes
of learning, rather than learning as an end point evaluation, Amy understands that
her plan will be modified as she gathers other data throughout the year.

Amy also has well-thought-out ideas about assessment. She believes that it
should support children's learning and involve self-reflection:

The instructional tools we design help us, as teachers, support children's learning
and assess our own teaching. After creating instruction of any kind, we then must be
reflective and ask ourselves: Is there a better way to ask that question? Can I teach that
skill another way? Should I pull a small group to revisit that concept? What did I say
that confused students so badly? Well, that worked well so can I incorporate that same
structure into other units? Did I assess a student on a genre she or he was unfamiliar

with? Why was that student unsuccessful with that text? It is not only my actual teaching that comes into play here, but my decision making as well.

These questions help Amy evaluate her instruction and reflect on children's learning behaviors relative to standards. They inform her decisions about new instructional moves that will focus on children's identified needs and help children better understand the learning process and themselves as learners.

For Amy, the teacher is the driving force of assessment, a model that is reflected in the SARW:

> Most educational assessment takes place in the classroom, as teachers and students interact with one another. Teachers design, assign, observe, collaborate in, and interpret the work of students in their classrooms. They assign meaning to interactions and evaluate the information that they receive and create in these settings. In short, teachers are the primary agents, not passive consumers, of assessment information. It is their ongoing, formative assessments that primarily influence students' learning. (p. 13)

A Classroom for Thinkers

Amy, in her third year of teaching, believes that she is:

> responsible for the learning environment, the energy that surrounds learning. I want children to be themselves and share their dreams and goals so that learning will be our joint purpose. I am responsible to help every child reach his or her potential, and that's lots of responsibility!

Amy's students begin their day with reading. They rush into the classroom, sharing news and insights from the previous afternoon and evening, unpack their book bags, get ready for the day, and read the morning message written on the whiteboard.

Child 1 (C1): Oh look, she did it again! That word should end in *ly*.

Child 2 (C2): No, it's okay to say, "Turn in your paper prompt."

C1: Oh. I didn't think we were talking about writing prompts.

C2: Yeah. Why would we turn in our writing prompts? We made them up for each other.

C1: Exactly! She means turn in your social studies work promptly. I bet so we won't be late for the book fair.

It is no accident that children in Amy's room notice words, look closely at language, and think about meaning. Children in this fifth-grade class enjoy daily read-alouds from texts such as *The Lost Hero* (Riordan, 2010), *Where the Red Fern Grows*

(Rawls, 1961), *Swine Not?* (Buffett, 2008), and *Martin's Big Words* (Rappaport, 2001). These are books that Amy suspects the children might not choose to read on their own. Each day, in a whole group, the children talk about their interpretations, confusions, wonderings, and feelings connected to the text that Amy reads aloud. The whole-group conversation ends with the children making predictions about what will happen next in the story. Amy records the children's predictions on a chart to hold their thoughts until the next day. This chart becomes an organically grown whole-group assessment tool that Amy uses to tailor the next day's instruction, ensuring that children's misconceptions and insights become focal points in the conversation.

Every day the children read independently. During this time, Amy meets with individual readers—she records each child's oral reading and retelling and checks for understanding by having conversations about books. She uses the anecdotal notes as an assessment strategy to monitor the growth of each reader in her class. Amy also uses these notes to better engage each child in conversations about the story and provide demonstrations of strategies to help each child understand what he or she is trying to accomplish while reading. In this way, each child learns how to use strategies and conversation to access the metacognitive processes involved in proficient reading. After independent reading, Amy and the children meet as a whole group to share strategies they used while reading and to talk about the way in which a particular strategy helped them make sense of text. Amy listens during whole-group discussion with the intention of using the children's thinking to name and extend their understandings of character traits, the story line, and the varied ways they use the text to make meaning of the story. In this way, Amy demonstrates how to analyze and synthesize the story; this further supports and guides children's thinking during independent reading.

Almost daily, children meet in small groups. Amy forms these groups based on patterns of needs and strengths she has identified in her anecdotal notes. Grouping children ensures that each child receives instruction based on need. Sometimes children meet in book clubs to talk about novels or facts they are learning in their social studies textbook. Other days they meet with Amy to get help on some aspect of the reading process. Amy listens in on the children's conversations, noting things they say or do, questions that need to be discussed, and any misconceptions. The children write in a variety of ways every day, including note-taking, exit slips, freewriting, and writer's notebooks.

Children lucky enough to be in this fifth-grade classroom are immersed in reading and writing and submerged in the real work of readers and writers. They do what needs to be done, singularly and collectively, to become more proficient readers and writers. Every day these children read, write, listen, and talk—not only to engage in story worlds but also to learn about the world and about themselves. In so doing, they build their capacity and skills for learning about reading and writing.

Data Inform Whole-Group Instruction

Amy uses data gathered from the children in small-group and one-on-one instruction to inform her plans for whole-group instruction. To gather it, she notices, listens, talks, and reflects. Consistent with the SARW, her assessment practices are valid because they "inform instruction and lead to improved teaching and learning" (p. 16). For example, based on observations she made when reading the children's memoirs, Amy decided to include the word *prompt* in an adverb slot during the morning message. Her decision was based on the children's needs, which she uncovered when she read their memoirs. Her morning message led the children to carefully explore and learn about the words they wanted to use in their own writing. When asked how, in her third year of teaching, she knew how to use data, Amy explained:

> In my college classes, I had professors that instilled the importance of data-driven instruction. I learned the value of using the information students provided to tailor my instruction to fit their needs, while still keeping my focus for instruction. Although learning about it and actually doing it are two different things, I was very fortunate to begin my teaching career in a school that valued instruction driven by data.

At the beginning of the school year, to help the children learn about language from the morning message, Amy read the message aloud each day and then prompted children with questions like, "What do you notice about punctuation? Do you notice any homophones? Do you know another way of spelling the short *o* sound? Can you think of a way to make that sentence sound better? Did you wonder why I underlined that phrase?" Through these kinds of questions, she intentionally led children on a journey into the ways of words, guiding them as they experimented with language and discovered the power of grammar, punctuation, and spelling. Amy explained that through this kind of daily demonstration, "By February, the children ask questions to scaffold one another and often challenge one another to learn in ways I never considered."

Amy not only learns from observing and recording children's thinking during whole-group, small-group, and one-on-one instruction, but she also asks children to name their learning through the use of exit slips. After an initial mini-lesson that used what children knew about reading fictional texts, for example, Amy gave them a genre exit slip. On it she asked them to "Explain the difference between fiction and nonfiction" and "Name three types of fiction and give an example of each." With these slips, she engaged children in the learning process while also learning about the children's needs, using this information to guide her plans for a unit on nonfiction. Based on her prior experience, she also knew that for children to learn to write well in the nonfiction genre, she needed to guide them in reading many nonfiction books. By doing this, she gave the children ample time to explore the genre and discover features common to it. About this whole-group assessment strategy, Amy noted:

> In our exploration of nonfiction, children noticed that short sentences were common, descriptive language was kept to a minimum, new vocabulary was often bolded or italicized, photographs and graphs were often used, and books often had an index. Using these discoveries, not only did children build a general and specific vision of what was possible in authoring nonfiction, but they had an opportunity to learn interesting information about the world.

To further understand what children have learned, Amy uses rubrics that require them to self-evaluate. She does this because she believes that, in assessing their own work, children uncover their own competencies and needs even as they are reminded about what they have learned. Amy also knows that self-assessment intentionally supports children's acquisition of and responsibility for a process that puts the child in charge of extending his or her own learning. Amy used this method after the whole-group study of nonfiction (see Figure 28). Rubrics also inform parents about content, strategies, and behaviors that are significant for learning and school success. Self-assessment components of the rubric reveal the child's view of his or her performance and provide fodder for parent–teacher conferences that often unite the adults in a quest to further the child's learning.

Amy explains how she constructs whole-group assessments:

> I think of three things when designing these whole-group assessments: (a) What I've learned about individual children during reading conferences—their strengths and needs, (b) state standards or the information others will hold children accountable for learning, and (c) what my instruction should look/sound like in order to build a strong bridge between what children currently know and what they need to know.

As noted in the SARW, planning to assess by "seeking multiple perspectives and multiple sources of data . . . takes advantage of the depth of understanding that various assessment procedures afford and the dialogue and learning they may produce" (p. 25).

Data Inform Small-Group Instruction

Amy uses data gathered from anecdotal notes taken during one-on-one reading conferences to plan specific small-group instruction or to address topics in small

Figure 28. A nonfiction scoring rubric.

Name _____ # _____
Due Date _____

"Nonfiction" self-writing	
What would I score myself?	**What my teacher scored me:**
***Note: If you did not give yourself full credit, change your writing!	
___/3- Rough draft: revisions and edits are obvious	___/3- Rough draft: revisions and edits are obvious
Writing:	Writing:
___/4- content: stays on topic and is fully supported	___/4- content: stays on topic and is fully supported
___/4- organization: organized by topics	___/4- organization: organized by topics
___/3- voice: use of third person and perspective and vocabulary	___/3- voice: use of third person and perspective and vocabulary
___/4- conventions: proper word endings and plurals, use of apostrophes, correct spelling of "no excuse" words, ending punctuation, beginning capital letters	___/4- conventions: proper word endings and plurals, use of apostrophes, correct spelling of "no excuse" words, ending punctuation, beginning capital letters
Publishing:	Publishing:
___/3- Effectively used at least 2 print features	___/3- Effectively used at least 2 print features
___/2- Effectively used at least 1 graphic feature	___/2- Effectively used at least 1 graphic feature
___/2- Effectively used at least 1 illustration	___/2- Effectively used at least 1 illustration
___/2- Effectively used at least 1 organizational feature	___/2- Effectively used at least 1 organizational feature
___/3- Includes 3 subheadings with a paragraph under each	___/3- Includes 3 subheadings with a paragraph under each
_____/30- Student comments:	_____/30- Teacher comments:

groups that she originally explored as a whole class. Early in the year, for example, data from the *Dominie* "Sentence Writing and Spelling Assessment" (DeFord, 2004) revealed that some children in her room needed additional support exploring how letter patterns affect spelling and word meaning. Based on children's writing and one-on-one reading conference data, Amy found that some other children needed to increase their understandings of literal and inferential meanings of words based on the story context and how authors, including themselves, intentionally use words to affect the meanings that readers glean from their texts. In October, Amy's anecdotal note data revealed that still other children needed support to understand that authors intentionally create visual images of characters and that change in characters' motives and personalities direct the story line or plot. Using these data, Amy developed instructional strategies to implement with the flexible small groups she created.

For example, Amy created a "Word Detectives" form (see Figure 29), based on the Latin word *detectus*, which means to "uncover or disclose." She told the children in one small group that each of them would become a word detective by using a portion of their independent reading and writing time to closely investigate word formations, discover ways words are used, and explore how words originated. Using the patterns of children's needs that she had identified early in the year,

Figure 29. Word detective chart.

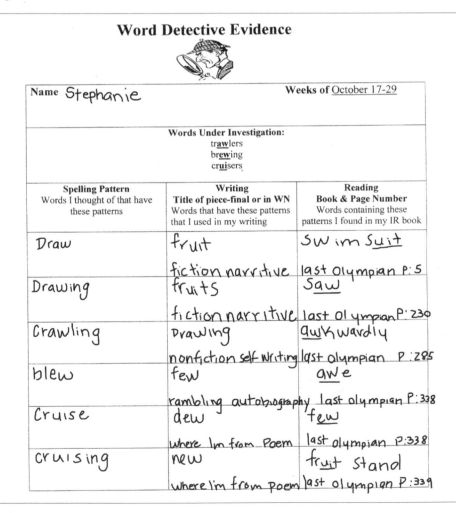

Word Detective Evidence

Name Stephanie		Weeks of October 17-29
Words Under Investigation: trawlers / brewing / cruisers		
Spelling Pattern Words I thought of that have these patterns	**Writing** Title of piece-final or in WN Words that have these patterns that I used in my writing	**Reading** Book & Page Number Words containing these patterns I found in my IR book
Draw	fruit / fiction narritive	swim suit / last Olympian p.5
Drawing	fruits / fiction narritive	saw / last Olympian P. 230
Crawling	Drawing / nonfiction self writing	awkwardly / last olympian P.285
blew	few / rambling autobiography	awe / last olympian P.338
Cruise	dew / where Im from Poem	few / last olympian P.338
cruising	new / where I'm from Poem	fruit stand / last olympian P.339

Amy challenged the children to develop their awareness of word construction and increase their wordsmithing capabilities. Similarly, in a small-group demonstration, Amy invited the children to explore the meaning of character in relation to story using *Enemy Pie* (Munson, 2000). For added practice, she asked the students to use their independent reading book to complete a character map and bring it to their next small-group discussion (see Figure 30). By using the open-ended word detective and character map frameworks, Amy gives children concrete scaffolds to reference and use as they deepen and expand their comprehension while reading independently. This helps them develop intellectual habits and reading strategies and supports their growing understandings of words and story worlds. It's clear that in Amy's classroom, assessment practices are responsive to children's changing

Figure 30. Character map.

Name Marcy Text Ron's Big Mission

Ron

Character Map

What does your character look like?

Black skin
Black hair
Young
Brow eyes

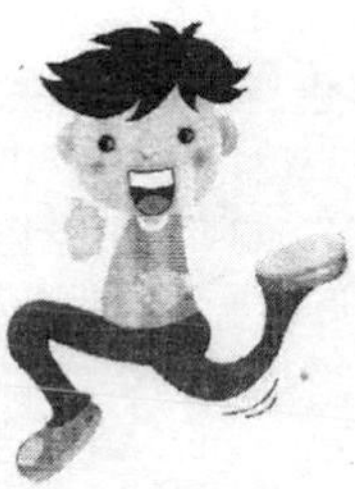

What does he/she act like?

He wants to check out his own books.
He will stand up for what he belives in.

How do others react to your character?

For each characteristic:

Mark **D** if you will tell us directly.

Mark **I** if we will learn about a characteristic indirectly.

I ·The mom smiled at her son.
I ·Ron says "I have to be some where"
D "I've got something impontant day."
I "Did'nt she here me?
D Mrs. Scott and the desk clerk did not know what to do.

needs and are designed to support learning, generate conversations, and inform the learner, teacher, and parent, rather than evaluating learning as a static end point.

One-on-One Reading Conferences Yield the Best Data

Each time Amy meets with children one on one or in guided reading groups, she takes anecdotal notes to learn about their attitudes toward reading, the genres they're exploring, and their current strategies and struggles. As she explains, "I use my anecdotal notes to help me plan instruction to better meet children's needs. These notes are the best way to find out what children do well, their individual needs, and how to group readers for strategy instruction."

In addition to finding out how well children understand what they read, Amy takes an informal miscue using a "skinny strip" (Stephens, 2005; see Figure 31), on which she numbers the miscues a student makes and marks Y(es), N(o), or P(artial) to indicate whether each miscue in the passage makes sense and whether it is graphically similar. Amy explains:

> I was introduced to the skinny strip in one of my graduate-level classes, "Instructional Strategies for Reading." After learning the value of the strip, we practiced on some sample reading assessments. I found that these strips were so beneficial in the reading classroom because they gave a quick overview to the cueing systems students were actively using. I immediately put this instructional tool to use in my reading classroom. By calculating a percentage, I could easily identify cues students needed to focus on, usually semantics. I was also able to speak to parents in a language they were able to understand, giving them a concrete example of how often their child relied on visual cues (looking at letters and sounds) or meaning cues (using the context of the story) to decode words.

One Reader's Story

Aliyan was home-schooled the year before entering the fifth grade. Her parents, concerned about the fact that she read below grade level, hired a tutor, who used the Orton-Gillingham program (www.ortongillingham.com). On August 27, Amy recorded in her anecdotal notes, "Ali seems very timid and self-conscious about her reading." Based on her analysis of Aliyan's oral reading and a Burke reading interview (Goodman, Watson, & Burke, 1987), Amy hypothesized that Aliyan seldom used meaning-based strategies when text she read didn't make sense. Instead, she consistently relied on grapho-phonic or visual cues; most frequently, she tried "breaking the word into smaller parts" or "looking at the first letter to guess the word." Based on her anecdotal notes from the first two weeks of school, Amy also hypothesized that Aliyan was not a confident reader.

Figure 31. Skinny strip based on oral reading of text.

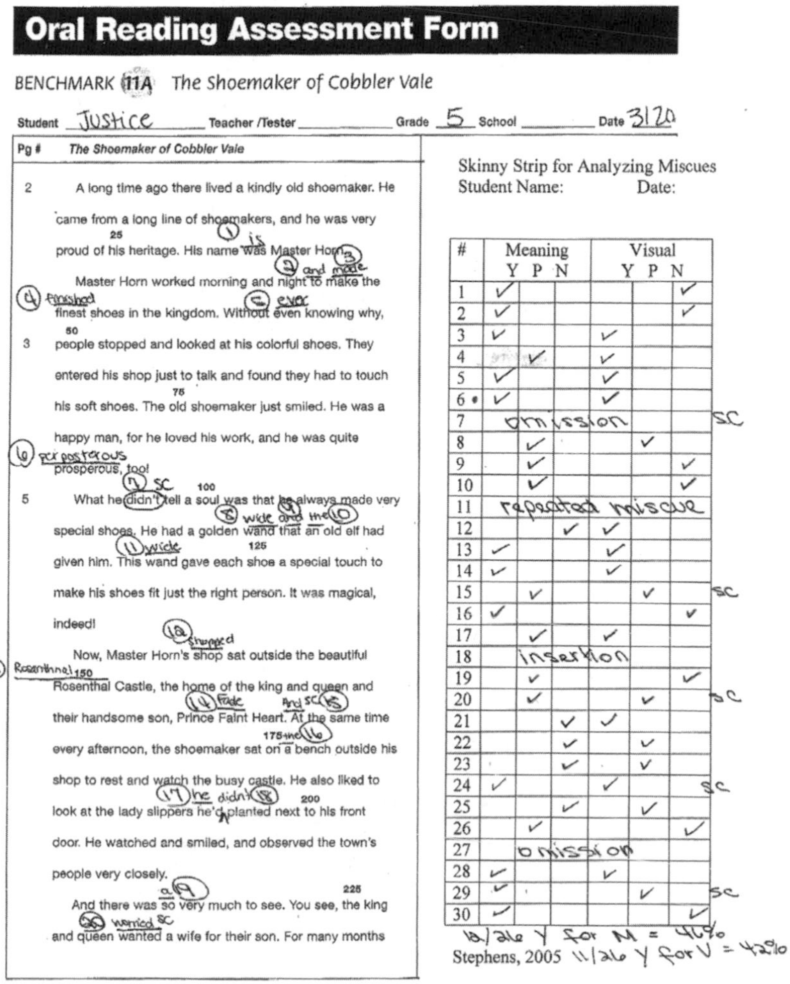

Oral Reading Assessment Form

BENCHMARK 11A *The Shoemaker of Cobbler Vale*

Student Justice Teacher /Tester ______ Grade 5 School ______ Date 3/20

Pg # *The Shoemaker of Cobbler Vale*

2 A long time ago there lived a kindly old shoemaker. He came from a long line of shoemakers, and he was very proud of his heritage. His name was Master Horn.

Master Horn worked morning and night to make the finest shoes in the kingdom. Without even knowing why,

3 people stopped and looked at his colorful shoes. They entered his shop just to talk and found they had to touch his soft shoes. The old shoemaker just smiled. He was a happy man, for he loved his work, and he was quite prosperous, too!

5 What he didn't tell a soul was that he always made very special shoes. He had a golden wand that an old elf had given him. This wand gave each shoe a special touch to make his shoes fit just the right person. It was magical, indeed!

Now, Master Horn's shop sat outside the beautiful Rosenthal Castle, the home of the king and queen and their handsome son, Prince Faint Heart. At the same time every afternoon, the shoemaker sat on a bench outside his shop to rest and watch the busy castle. He also liked to look at the lady slippers he'd planted next to his front door. He watched and smiled, and observed the town's people very closely.

And there was so very much to see. You see, the king and queen wanted a wife for their son. For many months

Skinny Strip for Analyzing Miscues
Student Name: Date:

#	Meaning Y	Meaning P	Meaning N	Visual Y	Visual P	Visual N	
1	✓					✓	
2	✓					✓	
3	✓			✓			
4		✓		✓			
5	✓			✓			
6 •	✓			✓			
7	omission						SC
8		✓			✓		
9		✓				✓	
10		✓				✓	
11	repeated miscue						
12			✓	✓			
13	✓			✓			
14	✓			✓			
15		✓			✓		SC
16	✓					✓	
17		✓		✓			
18	insertion						
19		✓				✓	
20		✓			✓		SC
21			✓	✓			
22			✓		✓		
23			✓		✓		
24	✓			✓			SC
25			✓		✓		
26		✓				✓	
27	omission						
28	✓			✓			
29	✓				✓		SC
30	✓					✓	

12/26 Y for M = 46%
Stephens, 2005 11/26 Y for V = 42%

In the third week of school, Amy met with Aliyan for the second time to learn more about her as a reader. In her reading folder, Aliyan had listed *Diary of a Wimpy Kid* as the only book she had read so far that year. While she did not identify which Wimpy Kid book she had read, most of the books in the series are written at about a 3.5 reading level. The text size is large and the books include picture cartoons. During this reading conference, Amy also learned that Aliyan had difficulty retelling a story and that she did not have many books at home.

Amy knew that to help Aliyan gain confidence as a reader and increase her comprehension she needed to encourage Aliyan to access semantic cues available in texts (such as using pictures and story context) while simultaneously helping her cross-check visual cues. Amy began to provide one-on-one and small-group instruction on meaning-making strategies (including skip the word and read on; reread; look at the picture and make predictions before, during, and after reading). As the year progressed, Aliyan's excitement about her reading progress showed in such statements as "Look how far I've gotten in this book" and "Let me tell you what's happened now!"

During this same time period, Aliyan expressed a desire to read *The Lightning Thief* (Riordan, 2005), a book written at about the seventh-grade level; it has complex story lines and multiple characters. Her parents offered to read the book aloud with her at home, and with her parents' support, Aliyan was able to participate in lively book club conversations about it with her peers. Through these conversations, Aliyan became engaged in talking about story characters and was soon immersed in the same story worlds that entertained her classmates.

In January, Amy suggested that Aliyan work with a reading interventionist. This would provide Aliyan with additional support and also provide Amy with another teacher's viewpoint. The two teachers could share data and work together to create lessons that would improve Aliyan's reading. The interventionist hypothesized that Aliyan was not yet spontaneously stopping when the text did not make sense. She encouraged her to "stop and think" after every paragraph about what was happening in the story. After a few weeks of practicing this strategy with the interventionist and in the classroom, Aliyan began monitoring her meaning-making as she read and reread when the text seemed confusing. During a March 17 reading conference with Aliyan, Amy noted that, after reading aloud a portion of her independent reading book, *Dog Whisperer: The Rescue* (Edwards, 2009), Aliyan gave a full and strong retelling. Amy's anecdotal notes on May 20 showed that Aliyan scored 90 percent comprehension on a *Dominie* (DeFord, 2004) Level 13 text, which has an equated level of 4.9. Amy was pleased with Aliyan's growth, as was Aliyan, who proudly stated three reasons for her reading success this year: (1) learning to pick a "just right" book, (2) talking about books (stories), and (3) learning to make inferences.

Aliyan's story demonstrates how Amy assessed Aliyan's needs through one-on-one conversations and small-group instruction and focused on those needs to facilitate Aliyan's literacy growth. Amy provides similar help for all of her students. Last year, of the twenty-two children in her class, fifteen readers met or exceeded standardized target goals; of the twenty readers who did not leave her class at any time during literacy instruction, nineteen showed growth on standardized measures. Amy notes that:

like Aliyan, the most significant growth was in children's confidence in their personal ability to talk about stories and strategically make sense of text. Children who believe they have tools to make sense of text confidently try to read increasingly harder books. It's exciting!

Final Words about Assessment

In Amy's classroom, assessment and instruction are integrated—assessment is a natural, ongoing part of classroom life. Amy believes that standardized tests are not the most useful data when trying to make a difference in children's daily learning lives. She prefers classroom-based assessments. As she explains:

> Assessments give me insight into what students know and what they still need to work on. [They] are tools to help me assess my own teaching . . . [and] improve my instruction. Assessments are windows into what a child is doing and learning in a classroom setting; therefore, they should yield valuable information that can be used to drive instruction without interrupting the learning environment.
>
> In every classroom, children have a wide variety of strengths and needs. In order to serve each child well, I must consider individual needs and strengths to create instruction that helps them process concepts and grow. This could mean modifying an assessment or changing the format of an assessment for a particular child or group of children. This also means considering the child's experiences and background knowledge when analyzing data from an assessment. Basically, it means being responsive.
>
> I believe that the most useful modes of assessment are those I create and use on a daily basis. These tools help me immediately see children's strengths and needs and keep my instruction focused on children's learning. I feel the pressure from the standardized tests imposed by state and federal lawmakers. Although I understand the need for whole-school accountability, these types of assessment give us little insight on the specific strengths and weaknesses of students. These tests are high-stakes, high-pressure tests that give results based in percentiles and RIT ranges. Very rarely are the results broken down to target specific skills or concepts. Many times, the scores of this type of assessment are given to us after students have already left our classes and are in their next year of schooling. This information is useful but I can't use it to revise my teaching for children.
>
> I believe that I need to always strive to get a complete picture of a child before making judgments. In my college literacy class, we learned about a holistic assessment model [Anthony, Johnson, Mickelson, & Preece, 1991] and that has stuck with me. Holistic assessment involves collecting multiple types of data (process notes, student work, standardized measures, and classroom rubrics) and analyzing all of them, as a whole, to get the full picture of one child. When looking at one child's reading, I use my own observations; informal miscues [Goodman, Watson, & Burke, 1987]; modification using skinny strips [Stephens, 2005]; DeFord's [2004] *Dominie* assessments; and standardized test data from MAP [Northwest Evaluation Association, 2011] and

PASS [Data Recognition Corporation, 2009]. I also use checklists to help me think about children's reading behaviors and stages of reading and inventories, like the Burke reading interview [Goodman, Watson, & Burke, 1987], to help get a picture of a child's beliefs about reading.

Amy understands that assessment practices should inform all stakeholders (students, parents, and the teacher), and she makes sure her students' parents are involved in this process:

> I try to include families in their children's assessments at various points of the year. At the beginning of the year, I send home an inventory asking parents to tell me about their child's likes and dislikes, strengths and weaknesses, and reading and writing habits. I use this information to help me stock my classroom library and get to know the kids. At the end of the year, I ask parents to explore their child's writing portfolios. During this time, children and parents work together to notice areas of growth and strengths and set goals based on what they see. This time usually feels like a grand celebration, even with needs being named. If parents are unavailable, I invite administrators or media specialists to ensure that each child has an adult to help review and celebrate his or her writing accomplishments. I believe that parents and teachers need to have ongoing communication. Narrative progress reports, coupled with a child's work and other assessments, show parents how well I know their child, as well as what can be done at home to assist their child in his or her learning quest. All parents want their children to succeed, but many don't know what to do to help them. Open, regular communication helps children grow in their literacy practices.

Conclusion

When individual readers and writers engage in the real work of reading and writing for the entire 180 days of the school year, they learn that reading and writing are tools they can use to learn about themselves, others, and the world. This work satisfies both child and teacher. Assessment data fuel this work and make it easy to ground instruction in a child's individual and common strengths and needs. When teachers understand standards as tools to help them envision curriculum and instruction, they learn to trust their own data-driven processes that connect responsive, thoughtful instruction to the needs of children. In classrooms like Amy's, teachers use a variety of data and feel a responsibility to use that information to imagine instruction that will help every child achieve his or her dreams. At the end of our time together, Amy offered this quote, which has made a difference in her life as a teacher: "[L]earning and reading are enhanced by teachers who know their students and their curriculum well and who use their knowledge of children to diversify instruction to meet their students' needs" (Calkins, Montgomery, & Santman, 1998, p. 6).

See Figure 32 for a list of assessment tools and instructional methods Amy uses in her classroom.

Figure 32. Classroom teacher Amy Oswalt's assessment tools and instructional moves.

Assessment Tools

Observation

Listening

Asking questions

Taking anecdotal notes

Exit slips

Dominie "Sentence Writing and Spelling" and "Text Reading"

Student self-evaluation

Skinny strips (version of miscue analysis)

MAP

PASS

Reflection

Informal miscue

Notes on children's genre selections

Review of children's writing samples (looking for well-crafted language, spelling, and grammar needs)

Comparison of children's progress with state standards

Instructional Moves

Customized engagements for children based on data (e.g., morning message).

Developed mini-lessons.

Provided strategy instruction.

Conducted whole-group strategy share to spotlight children's individual strategies.

Matched children and texts.

Formed flexible small groups based on instructional need.

Customized instruction to teach group.

Arranged supplemental support as needed.

Asked parents to read aloud to child.

Picked texts for read-alouds and classroom library.

Provided time for reading.

Provided access to books.

Provided time for talk about books.

Note

   1. South Carolina's ABC Child Care Voucher Program is a voluntary program that helps qualifying families pay for child care so they can work. For information, go to http://www.childcare.sc.gov.

Making a Difference

The twelve classroom teachers in the cases and portraits you just read are all making a difference in the lives of the children with whom they work.

For years, the field of reading education has been debating whether one method of reading instruction is superior to another. At the same time, research has shown again and again (and again) that it is the teacher, not the method, that makes a difference (see, for example, Anderson, Hiebert, Scott, & Wilkinson, 1985; Bond & Dykstra, 1967/1997; Crismore, 1985; Darling-Hammond, 2000; Duffy, 1983; Duffy, Roehler, & Putnam, 1987; Ferguson, 1991; Langer, 2000; National Center for Education Statistics, 1994; Sanders, 1988 Sipay, 1968).

This idea of teachers making a difference has been explored in a series of studies known as "best practice" studies (see, for example, Allington & Johnston, 2000; Morrow, 2002; Pressley, Rankin, & Yokoi, 1996; Taylor, 2002; Taylor, Pearson, Clark, & Walpole, 2000; Taylor, Pearson, Peterson, & Rodriguez, 2003; Wharton-McDonald, Pressley, & Hampston, 1998). In these studies, researchers have expanded on the still-accepted ideas laid out in *Becoming a Nation of Readers* (Anderson et al., 1985), whose authors argued that effective teachers:

- Provide extensive time for children to read often and to read a wide range of authentic literature: "Research suggests that the amount of independent, silent reading children do in school is significantly related to gain in reading achievement" (p. 76).

- Provide ample books and ready access to those books: such books should be well written and matched to the student's strengths (pp. 43–48, 62–65).

- Help students make connections between their background knowledge and the text (pp. 49–51).

- Read aloud to students: "The single most important activity for building the knowledge required for eventual success in reading is reading aloud to children" (p. 23).

- Provide extensive time for children to write: writing contributes to "growth in phonics, spelling, vocabulary development, and reading comprehension" (p. 79).

Many of these findings were echoed in the 1992 NAEP analysis of fourth-grade data (National Center for Education Statistics, 1994). The report found that the following practices correlate positively with higher scores: (a) the use of trade books as opposed to basal readers, (b) a heavy emphasis on reading and writing instead of workbooks and worksheets, (c) literature-based approaches that focus on comprehension and interpretation as opposed to teaching subskills, (d) weekly trips to the library, and (e) weekly use of written assignments to assess reading as opposed to multiple-choice or short-answer tests.

Characteristics that have subsequently been added to the list of best practices include classrooms filled with print; teacher modeling; individualized as well as small-group instruction (Pressley et al., 1996); teaching self-regulation; integrating reading and writing into content areas (Wharton-McDonald et al., 1998); using data to form small groups (Taylor et al., 2000); teacher assessment; flexible use of materials, strategies, and talk as a means of communication; conducting inquiry; building trust (Allington & Johnston, 2001); and an emphasis on higher-order thinking (Taylor et al., 2003).

It is clear to me and to many in the field, however, that classrooms that really work—that feel like great places for children and teachers as readers, writers, and learners—are united by more than just these characteristics. Robin W. Cox, coauthor of the third-grade portrait, has been conducting research on this topic (Cox, 2012). In her job as elementary language arts instructional specialist for her district, she noticed that some best practice teachers were able to help their students significantly increase their ability to handle more complex texts; other best practice teachers did not have the same impact. To understand what might account for this difference, Robin reviewed the literature, constructed a list of best practices (see Figure 33), and asked principals, literacy coaches, and reading interventionists to use the list to nominate best practice third-grade teachers.

Figure 33. Characteristics of best practice teachers.

Best Practices Rubric

Directions: Please rate your third grade teachers on this rubric. Use the following rating scale:
1=absence of evidence, 2=some evidence, 3=mostly evident, 4=always evident

Descriptor	No info available	1 absence of evidence	2 some evidence	3 mostly evident	4 always evident
Classroom Organization • Spaces for whole group, small group, and independent work are provided. • Materials are organized and available for student use. • Student desks are arranged to allow for collaboration. • Anchor charts are created with students and are displayed for student use. • Student work is displayed. • The classroom is filled with print.					
Classroom Climate/Language • Student responses are valued and encouraged. • Students work with one another in a respectful manner. • The teacher uses coaching language with students. • The teacher is explicit in his/her instructional language. • The teacher asks high-ordered questions, encouraging analysis, synthesis, and evaluation. • The teacher provides explicit demonstrations for comprehension and decoding strategies.					
Reading Workshop: Independent Reading • Time is devoted daily to independent reading. • The teacher confers with students. • The teacher begins workshop or independent reading with a mini-lesson. • The teacher allows for sharing of strategies and ideas. • There are a variety of texts on varying levels for students to read. • Students have access to books. • The teacher ensures that students are matched to their levels.					
Reading Workshop: Shared Reading • Shared reading is used on a regular basis to demonstrate strategies. • A variety of texts and genres are used for shared reading.					
Reading Workshop: Read Aloud • The teacher reads aloud three to four times daily. • The teacher reads aloud for many purposes (enjoyment, introduce a genres, think-aloud for strategy instruction, elicit student responses/discussion, share new books) • The teacher reads from a variety of genres and varying texts.					
Reading Workshop: Small Groups • The teacher has small groups frequently (3-5 times per week). • When employing guided reading, the teacher guides students in the text and observes students' use of strategies. • Small groups are used for response to literature study/discussion, as well as guided practice.					
Writing • Students write in response to reading. • Students write for a variety of purposes. • The teacher provides daily/ample time to write.					
Assessment • The teacher uses text reading as a regular part of her assessment. • The teacher knows how to analyze records and does so. • The teacher uses assessment data to inform instruction. • The teacher uses kidwatching as a part of her assessment.					

2

-developed by Robin W. Cox, July 2010

Robin subsequently interviewed two of the nominated third-grade teachers from each school (a total of six teachers from three Title I schools). She interviewed them once before the beginning of the school year, a second time after four classroom observations (two in the fall and two in the spring), and once more at the end of the year. The patterns she found are enlightening. Best practice teachers who were making a difference, both in terms of reading-level growth on the *Dominie* (DeFord, 2004) and standardized test scores (MAP, Northwest Evaluation Association, 2011), shared the following characteristics:

1. They had excellent classroom management skills.
2. They used talk to help students develop identities as readers and writers.
3. They named their beliefs about readers and reading.
4. Their practices were aligned with their beliefs.
5. Their instruction was focused.
6. They endeavored to know each child as a reader and they used the data they collected to inform instruction.

The teachers featured in this volume have all of these characteristics. They use their considerable classroom management skills to create learning communities in which every child feels "at home"—loved, supported, taken care of, noticed, and celebrated. They think about how they talk to children to ensure that they send the message that their students are readers and writers. Through talk, they help children understand that they have agency. These twelve teachers also have a clear sense of "what matters" about readers and reading, and their practices are consistent with those beliefs.

What may not be as obvious at first glance is that their instruction is also focused. In each "lesson," each conversation, these teachers are trying to help students learn *one new thing*. This is in stark contrast to guided reading protocols in which teachers try to address a multitude of skills in twenty or thirty minutes. In such lessons, students do not have an opportunity to learn the one thing they next need to know. Especially for struggling readers, these jam-packed events must feel like James's "blooming, buzzing confusion" (James, 1890, p. 488).

Finally, all the teachers in this volume have systematic ways of collecting data about children. They then use that data to inform instruction. Their assessment tools are described in the narratives and listed in tables at the end of each case study and portrait. Looking across these portraits, I recognize many similarities in terms of the assessment tools they employ (see Figure 34).

By watching and listening, all of the teachers notice every child. This seems like a simple task—it is not. I teach reading assessment courses, and I consistently

---

Figure 34. Artful teachers' strategies for assessing students.

Artful teachers:

1. Watch, listen, and notice each child
2. Ask questions to help children understand more fully
3. Make use of a variety of assessment tools
4. Find a systematic way to record and reflect on their observations
5. Engage children in self-assessment.

---

ask teachers to record what they saw or heard a child do or say. Following are a few examples of the observations teachers shared with me:

- When "A," a second grader, was reading a below-grade-level text and came to the word *cricket*, she stopped and looked away from the book. When I asked her what she was doing, she said she was thinking about word chunks. She continued to look away for a few moments, then held up her two index fingers, looked at the book for several moments, and said, "I found one." She put her fingers around *ri*.

- When I asked "B," a fourth grader, to read *Pigsty* (Teague, 1994, level 2.8), she read the line, "They rolled up his blankets and hogged his pillows too." She then said, "Get it? Hogged? Because they are pigs." Later in the book, she read the line, "Wendall told himself he didn't mind but then he found footprints on his comic books." She then said, "Oh no."

- When I brought in a number of books today and asked "C," a fifth grader, to sort into piles the books she would and would not want to read, she picked *Freedom School, Yes!* (Littlesugar, 2001, level 3.5). When I asked her why, she said, "It's in my range." Her reading, though, was choppy, and she began squirming and playing with her zipper.

These are specific observations. However, often (and with the best intentions) teachers in my classes initially write down not what they noticed, but what they *thought* about what they saw and heard. Some examples:

- "[She was] very verbal, but it sometimes takes her a while to get her thoughts out."
- "The usual thing is that he can answer comprehension questions even if he has used incorrect words."
- "Her vocabulary is weak."
- "She uses the 'Eagle strategy' when she gets to a word she doesn't know. She does not use the other strategies at this time."

Experienced teachers make hundreds of quick decisions every day. They notice and almost instantaneously make a judgment and then act. This quick thinking is essential to a well-run classroom. At the same time, quick judgments sometimes make it hard to systematically notice what students are saying and doing and record that information in such a way that it can be reflected on later. Eventually, teachers in my classes begin to write down exactly what they see and hear. This helps them better understand children as readers, writers, and learners—but it takes time and practice.

The twelve teachers featured in this book have honed their skills of observation and listening. Lee recorded, for example, that "Rosalee said, when she came to a word she didn't know, she 'split the word up.' She looked at the end of the word first and then the beginning of the word, and put it all together." Really hearing what Rosalee said helped Lee think about what Rosalee, a third grader, knew and how she thought. Similarly, when Tammy asked her preschoolers what they wanted to know about birds, she wrote down their questions verbatim. She did so because she understood that having that written record would allow her to reflect at the end of the day and think carefully about all of her students and the stances they were taking toward their inquiry.

All of these teachers ask questions that will help them better understand the child. When I was taking courses on Piaget several years ago, my professor, Herb Ginsberg, told the class that people studying with Piaget spent a year learning to ask questions. Questions needed to be contingent on what the other person said, open-ended, and phrased in such a way that they caused the child to reflect. The case studies and portraits in this book contain many examples of teachers asking such questions, including:

- Kathy asked David how he felt when she used the *Dominie* (DeFord, 2004) texts.

- Tim asked Cameron how she figured out the word *skip*.

- Erika asked her students to tell her what kind of reader they were that day.

These questions seem simple and "easy," and in many ways they are. They are a natural part of the inquiry-based conversations we all have with family and friends: "How was your day?" "What did you do at school?" "How did you work that problem out with your coworker/friend?" Teachers, though, are not accustomed to having inquiry-based conversations with children; we usually ask questions for which we already know the answer, and we most often talk to tell rather than to learn. It takes a while to shift from telling to learning and from looking for "right answers" to trying to understand, to conceptualize teaching as an inquiry-based conversation. The teachers featured in this volume have worked hard to make this shift.

***All twelve teachers use a variety of assessment tools; they know that one
tool cannot tell a complete story.*** Their tools include parent questionnaires, work
samples, checklists, anecdotal records, and tasks like the "Show Me Book" from
the *Dominie* (DeFord, 2004). Teachers of preschoolers who are not yet reading
conventionally sometimes integrate into the curriculum tasks that will provide
them with data. Tammy, for example, asks her three-, four-, and five-year-olds to
put their felt doll under either "school lunch" or "lunch box" labels. She tells them
stories and, in so doing, assesses their oral comprehension.

The teachers of children whose reading is more conventional have some additional tools (e.g., miscue analysis, running records, the Burke interview [Good-
man, Watson, & Burke, 1987], exit slips). They listen to children read and take
notes about children's cue use. Are the children predicting using meaning? Cross-
checking using visual information? Do they seem to understand that reading is
about making sense of print? Do they find reading pleasurable? Do they have the
skills and strategies needed to problem-solve when reading?

***All twelve teachers have a systematic way of recording and reflecting on
their own observations.*** Anne records her information on a hypothesis–test sheet
(Stephens, 1990; Stephens et al., 1996; Stephens & Story, 2000) and then considers interpretations and hypotheses grounded in what she has noticed. Kristy and
Ryan use Johnson's (2006) "Here's What, So What, Now What, Then What"
framework. Louise takes anecdotal notes during the day and in the evening uses
them as the basis for reflective memos. Erika creates literacy profiles. Each of these
teachers has developed a system that suits her well. Again, this takes time. Teachers
need to work out what they want to keep track of and then come up with a way that
meshes well with their ways of being. I am reminded of a teacher friend of mine
whose classroom was what I would consider messy. I am forever organizing; she
was content to just let things be. But she sure knew her kids. Her system? She carried sticky notes in her pocket and also had supplies of them all around the room.
At the end of the day, she stuck the numerous notes she had written onto a page
she kept for each student. There is never one right way to keep track of one's students—what matters is that each teacher develops a way that works for him or her.

All of these teachers engage children in self-assessment. This takes different
forms with different age levels of children. Tammy, for example, develops a lesson
to help the children become metacognitively aware that reading is a meaning-making process. Louise encourages her kindergartners to notice what they do as readers, writers, and learners and to write her notes about what they have done. She
and Tim both have a strategy-sharing time in which the children report what they
notice about themselves as readers. Sandy begins the year with a lesson on metacognition and expects her third graders to all eventually be able to name what they
do as readers. Erika lets her students know she is watching them, and she expects

them to be watching themselves. Amy develops a variety of reflective worksheets that help students become increasingly self-aware. Helping students become self-aware is essential. It is part of Pearson and Gallagher's (1983) gradual release of responsibility model: students come to understand what it is they need to know and be able to do and gradually take over full responsibility for doing so. They acquire agency, and as Johnson (2006) notes, agency is necessary for continual growth.

These teachers do all these things—notice, ask, use a variety of assessment tools, systematically reflect, and engage children in self-reflection—with one overarching goal: they seek to develop a theory of each child as reader, writer, and learner. They know their theory is solid when it allows them to predict a child's behavior and responses. With such theories in place, teachers are positioned to provide instruction that will make a difference. They choose from among the best practices defined in the literature and develop their own practices—practices customized to the needs of individual children, to small groups of children, and, as applicable, to their class as a whole.

Without such theories, no matter how well-intentioned teachers may be, instruction is not closely targeted to need and so limits the progress students can make. This does not imply that these twelve teachers have reached some sort of pinnacle of teaching. All of them will tell you that they know more today than they knew yesterday, and that tomorrow they will know even more. This can happen for them because they have a strong and deep knowledge base about readers, reading, and children's literature; a vision of assessment as inquiry; and a commitment to using data to build a theory of each child and using that to inform instruction. Perhaps most important, they are determined to "outgrow . . . their former selves" (Harste, Woodward, & Burke, 1984)

In all of these ways, the twelve teachers showcased here live the *Standards for the Assessment of Reading and Writing* (IRA–NCTE, 2010): they marry assessment to instruction and make a difference in the lives of children.

Annotated Bibliography: Outgrowing Our Former Selves

The teachers in this volume are, indeed, all artful teachers. Some of them, such as Sandy Anfin and Amy Oswalt, are relative newcomers to this art; others, like Tim O'Keefe and Louise Ward, have more than thirty years of experience. All of them, though, ground what they do in their informed understandings about assessment, reading, writing, instruction, and children's literature. The texts they read, combined with their ongoing experiences and reflections, help them outgrow their former selves. In this annotated bibliography, the teachers heard and discussed in this book share with readers the articles and books they have found most helpful. Their hope is that these texts will likewise be helpful to other teachers.

For an extended annotated bibliography of great teacher resources, see https://secure.ncte.org/store/books/series/pip/stephensbib.

Learning about Assessment
(Diane E. DeFord and Lucy K. Spence)

Learning about Observation, Assessment, and Decision Making

Matteson, David M., and Deborah K. Freeman.
Assessing and Teaching Beginning Writers: Every Picture Tells a Story.
Katonah, NY: Owen, 2005. Print.

Designed for prekindergarten and early primary teachers, this book diagrams a continuum that assesses what very young children know about oral language, drawing, and writing. This easy-to-use tool helps teachers determine instruction and next literacy steps for their youngest students. The book includes writing and drawing samples, vignettes of best practice teacher–child conversations, and useful observation forms to help educators in early literacy settings easily record observations and design appropriate instruction.

Matteson, David M., and Deborah K. Freeman.
Assessing and Teaching Beginning Readers: A Picture Is Worth 1000 Words.
Katonah, NY: Owen, 2006. Print.

Writing again for prekindergarten and early primary teachers, Matteson and Freeman offer reading reenactments as a comprehensive approach to working with fiction and nonfiction texts. They also explore ways to develop children's oral language and help them learn how to look at and use print in the first books they read.

Mills, Heidi, with Tim O'Keefe.
"Inquiry into Assessment Strategies: From Kidwatching to Responsive Teaching."
Talking Points 22.2 (2011): 2–8. Print.

Mills and O'Keefe describe assessment strategies within a culture of inquiry in a classroom at the Center for Inquiry in Columbia, South Carolina. Teachers at the center use the naturally occurring data they collect and interpret as an ongoing part of rich literacy curriculum and instructional practices. The authors detail how they gather and interpret both formal and informal assessments and tailor instruction to meet the students' needs.

O'Keefe, Tim.
"Teachers as Kidwatchers."
Creating Classrooms for Authors and Inquirers. 2nd ed.
Ed. Kathy G. Short and Jerome C. Harste, with Carolyn Burke.
Portsmouth, NH: Heinemann, 1996. 63–80. Print.

This chapter in Short and Harste's excellent book defines *kidwatching* and describes how it is used in every aspect of the classroom, including journals, writing workshop, inquiry, parent partnerships, and the reading process itself. O'Keefe provides

a practical approach to assessment from the perspective of a practicing teacher.

Richardson, Jan.
**The Next Step in Guided Reading: Focused
Assessments and Targeted Lessons for Help-
ing Every Student Become a Better Reader.**
New York: Scholastic, 2009. Print.

Richardson lays out the components of an effective guided reading lesson—targeted assessments,
strategy instruction, and guided writing. The
book is divided into three stages of reading development for early, transitional, and fluent readers.
It offers suggestions for classroom structures and
provides information on grouping for guided
reading.

Strickland, Kathleen, and James Strickland. (1999).
Making Assessment Elementary.
Portsmouth, NH: Heinemann, 2000. Print.

There are so many things to take away from
this book, which includes sections on anecdotal
records, retrospective miscue analysis, surveys and
responses, and portfolios. The authors draw on
stories from schools across the country to describe
how to make assessment and instruction meaningful within the constraints imposed on schools.

Wilde, Sandra, ed.
**Notes from a Kidwatcher: Selected Writings
of Yetta M. Goodman.**
Portsmouth, NH: Heinemann, 1996. Print.

The twenty-three articles in this book chronicle
original work on the concept of *kidwatching*, a
term originally coined by Goodman. Particularly
relevant are Chapters 16 and 17: "Kidwatching:
An Alternative to Testing" and "Kidwatching:
Observing Children in the Classroom."

Learning to Describe and Analyze Reading

Goodman, Yetta M., Dorothy J. Watson, and Carolyn
L. Burke.
**Reading Miscue Inventory: From Evaluation
to Instruction. 2nd ed.**
Katonah, NY: Owen, 2005. Print.

This revised edition of *Reading Miscue Inventory*
details miscue analysis procedures and describes
reliable ways to analyze reading using miscues.
The book offers help in interpreting and using the
classic 1980 Burke reading inventory and provides
analyses of readers with different strengths and
challenges. It also provides guidance on instructional decision making.

     See also Goodman, Yetta M., and Caro-
lyn L. Burke. *Reading Miscue Inventory Manual:
Procedure for Diagnosis and Evaluation*. New York:
Macmillan, 1972. Print.

Wilde, Sandra.
**Miscue Analysis Made Easy: Building on
Student Strengths.**
Portsmouth, NH: Heinemann, 2000. Print.

Wilde explains how systems of meaning, language,
and graphic information work during reading and
suggest how teachers can help students grow as
readers. She also provides guidance on diagnostic
procedures, retelling guides, maximizing student
strengths, and ways to support comprehension.

Learning to Describe and Analyze Writing

Clay, Marie M.
How Very Young Children Explore Writing.
Portsmouth, NH: Heinemann, 2010. Print.

Clay discusses the concepts that children explore
when they first take pencil, crayon, or paint to
paper, such as learning about the size and shapes
of different letters and the difference between
pictures and print. She also includes information
about the patterns that children begin to notice
about print and the connection between print and
spoken words.

Clay, Marie M.
The Puzzling Code.
Portsmouth, NH: Heinemann, 2010. Print.

The Puzzling Code is written for teachers, parents, and caregivers of young children. It uses colorful images of children's writing and easy-to-understand language to present ways that teachers and parents can observe, assess, and record developments in young children's writing.

Spence, Lucy K.
"Discerning Writing Assessment: Insights into an Analytical Rubric."
Language Arts 87.5 (2010): 337–52. Print.

Spence presents a case study of three Spanish-speaking students in a third-grade classroom and posits that analytical rubrics may not be the best assessment tool for all children.

Spence, Lucy K.
"Generous Reading: Seeing Students through Their Writing."
Reading Teacher 63.8 (2010): 634–42. Print.

This article details an assessment process that looks carefully at a student's writing to reveal how she or he uses background knowledge when composing. The author offers suggestions on how to use the resulting findings to inform instruction.

Wong-Kam, JoAnn, Alice K. Kimura, Anna Y. Sumida, Joyce Ahuna-Ka'ai'ai, and Mikilani Hayes Maeshiro.
"Building Progress Folios: Documenting Growth over Time." Chapter 3.
Elevating Expectations: A New Take on Accountability, Achievement, and Evaluation.
Portsmouth, NH: Heinemann, 2001. 24–42. Print.

In this chapter, the authors present a folio system for assessing student writing, which they developed to promote critical evaluation of a student's own performance, and explain how to assemble it. They include photographs, examples of student work, and helpful suggestions for critical self-evaluation.

Assessment Tools for Emergent and Early Readers and Writers

Clay, Marie M.
Concepts about Print: What Have Children Learned about the Way We Print Language?
Portsmouth, NH: Heinemann, 2000. Print.

Marie Clay's Concepts about Print task allows teachers to observe what children notice about the way language is printed in books and in the environment. Using books by Clay such as *Follow Me, Moon; Sand* and *Stones;* and *No Shoes,* the child helps the teacher by pointing to certain features as the teacher reads. The teacher can then assess the child's knowledge in many areas.

Matteson, David M.
***The Emergent Reading Assessment: Assessing Three- to Five-Year-Olds* [part of assessment package].**
Katonah, NY: Owen, 2007. Print.

Matteson illustrates what three- to five-year-old children know about reading and provides insights for instruction. This book serves as a tool to help teachers observe and record their observations of book handling, print, and story concepts and then use this information to design appropriate reading instruction.

Learning More about Decision Making for English Learners

Ascenzi-Moreno, Laura, Cecilia M. Espinosa, Sarah Ferholt, Michael Loeb, Berky Lugo-Salcedo, and Cecelia Traugh.
"Learning through Descriptive Inquiry at the Cypress Hills Community School."
Language Arts 85.5 (2008): 392–400. Print.

This article explains how the authors worked through a collaborative descriptive inquiry group to broaden their understanding of bilingual children's literacy and literacy practices in order to support their development.

Gottlieb, Margo.
Assessing English Language Learners: Bridges from Language Proficiency to Academic Achievement.
Thousand Oaks, CA: Corwin, 2006. Print.

This volume contains a comprehensive overview of assessment for English learners, including a background on language acquisition and examples of assessments that can be used with such students. Chapter 5, "Classroom Assessment: The Bridge to Educational Parity," is particularly relevant for teachers implementing RTI.

Young, Terrell A., and Nancy L. Hadaway, eds.
Supporting the Literacy Development of English Learners: Increasing Success in All Classrooms.
Newark, DE: IRA, 2006. Print.

This text is designed to help teachers overcome common misconceptions about English learners and illustrates how to develop curriculum that meets the individual needs of these students. The authors discuss reading comprehension and show how demonstration and think-aloud help learners develop competencies in English reading. Particularly helpful are the specific instructional engagements designed to address key needs of English learners. The book also covers expository text structures, writing, and oral language.

Learning about the Reading Process (Diane Stephens)

Anderson, Richard C., Elfrieda H. Hiebert, Judith A. Scott, and Ian A. G. Wilkinson.
Becoming a Nation of Readers. The Report of the Commission on Reading.
Washington, DC: National Institute of Education, 1985. Print.

The authors of this report took on the task of synthesizing a review of the reading research literature conducted from the 1960s to the 1980s. While there was some debate about who was *not* on the panel, this report is a classic and makes explicit what was news then but is widely accepted now—that "reading is the process of constructing meaning from written texts."

Clay, Marie M.
Reading: The Patterning of Complex Behavior.
Portsmouth, NH: Heinemann, 1979. Print.

In her first book, Clay shares her extensive work with young readers and introduces her approach to classifying "reading errors" as visual, meaning, or syntax. She is best known for her assessment of young readers and for the development of Reading Recovery, an intervention approach that is designed to accelerate the progress of first graders before they fail as readers.
See also Clay, M. (1982). *Observing young readers*; Clay, M. (1991). *Becoming literate*; and Clay, M. (1998). *By different paths to common outcomes.*

Goodman, Kenneth S.
"Reading: A Psycholinguistic Guessing Game."
Journal of the Reading Specialist 6 (1967): 126–35. Print.

As a doctoral student at UCLA, Ken Goodman came to the realization that reading was not being conceptualized as language and, as an assistant professor at Wayne State University, began using descriptive linguistics to study reading. Among his many insights was the idea that readers use cue systems (grapho-phonemic, semantic, and syntax) when problem-solving words. He considered deviations from the text to be *miscues* that provide a window into the reading process. Goodman also hypothesized (and later demonstrated) that readers use information from the context, the text, and their experience (semantic and pragmatic cues), as well as syntactical cues, to predict words, and then use grapho-phonemic information to confirm those predictions.
(Reprinted in Singer, Harry, and Robert B. Ruddell, eds. *Theoretical Models and Processes of Reading*. 2nd ed. Newark, DE: IRA, 497–508. Print). *As of this printing, this article can be found online at https://uascentral.uas.alaska.edu/onlinelib/*

Fall-2007/ED674-JD1/Goodman_article.pdf. See also Goodman, Yetta M., Dorothy J. Watson, and Carolyn L. Burke. *Reading Strategies: Focus on Comprehension.* 2nd ed. Katonah, NY: Owen, 1996. Print. (1st ed. 1980) and Goodman, Kenneth S. "A Linguistic Study of Cues and Miscues in Reading." *Elementary English* 42.6, (1965): 639–43.

Smith, Frank.
Reading without Nonsense. 4th ed.
New York: Teachers College Press, 2006. Print.

In this fourth edition of *Reading without Nonsense,* Frank Smith explains that children learn to read as a consequence of trying to makes sense of print and their environment. He contends that it is not necessary to say what a word is to comprehend its meaning and that recognizing the meaning of something always comes before giving a name to it. Smith believes that children learn to read by gradually taking over the reading themselves and recommends that teachers provide children with opportunities to make sense of language in meaningful circumstances. He argues that "[t]he two basic necessities for learning to read are the availability of interesting material that makes sense to the learner and an understanding and more experienced reader as a guide."

Weaver, Constance.
Reading Process and Practice: From Socio-Psycholinguistics to Whole Language.
Portsmouth, NH: Heinemann, 1988. Print.

While *Becoming a Nation of Readers* provides a brief (120 page) overview of the major understandings about reading that are still current today, Weaver offers a closer look at that knowledge base, expanding it to include authors such as Clay, Goodman, and Smith, whose work was not cited in the Commission on Reading report. Weaver's text supplies teachers with information that they can use immediately to improve reading assessment and instruction.

Learning about Creating Classrooms for Readers
(Robin W. Cox, Anne Downs, Jennie Goforth, Lisa Jaegar, Ashley Matheny, Kristi Plyler, Lee Riser, Beth Sawyer, Tara Thompson, Kathy Vickio, and Cindy Wilcox)

Allington, Richard L.
What Really Matters for Struggling Readers: Designing Research-Based Programs.
New York: Longman, 2001. Print.

Allington examines the design and delivery of effective literacy instruction based on current research. This book is intended to help teachers create more effective interventions for struggling readers as Allington identifies and examines what matters most: reading volume, access to books, reading fluency, and developing thoughtful literacy.

Crowley, Paul.
"Listening to What Readers Tell Us."
Voices from the Middle 2.2 (1995): 3–12. Print.

Using authentic classroom examples, Paul Crowley brings his expertise as professor and former middle school reading teacher to demonstrate how teachers can become better-informed observers of readers. By comparing actual text passages to student miscues, he provides clear explanations of information gathered about the student reader and discusses the decision making involved in moving from miscue analysis to providing appropriate instruction. Other helpful information includes retrospective miscue analysis, reader-selected miscues, naming strategy, selected deletions, and writing to support reading. This article meets the needs of elementary and middle school reading teachers as well as reading interventionists.

Doake, David B.
"Reading-Like Behavior: Its Role in Learning to Read."
Observing the Language Learner.
Ed. Angela Jaggar and M. Trika Smith-Burke. Newark, DE: IRA; Urbana, IL: NCTE, 1985. 82–98. Print.

Doake details how "reading-like behaviors" develop in children due to the experiences provided by parents and teachers. He illustrates how children become actively involved in the process as they learn to read and shows how this understanding helps teachers and the decisions they make within their classroom support the growth of readers and learners.

Flurkey, Alan D.
"Taking Another Look at (Listen to) Shari."
Primary Voices K–6 3.4 (1995): 10–15. Print.

Flurkey discusses how learning miscue analysis shifted his beliefs about reading and deepened his understanding of the strengths and needs of his students. Before learning miscue analysis, Flurkey viewed reading as a process of reading all the words correctly and without difficulty. After learning miscue analysis, his thinking shifted to the belief that reading is a process of making sense of the text.

Fox, Mem.
Reading Magic: Why Reading Aloud to Our Children Will Change Their Lives Forever.
New York: Harcourt, 2001. Print.

Mem Fox outlines the tremendous and joyful literacy experience that children gain from listening to adults as they read books aloud. This book is written from Fox's perspective as a mother as well as from her experiences as an author and literacy consultant. Fox offers practical advice for parents and teachers on how to read aloud to children to achieve literacy growth. She also provides an understanding of the importance of hearing language and how it is foundational to later reading success.

Hood, Wendy J.
"I Do Teach and the Kids Do Learn."
Primary Voices K–6 3.4 (1995): 16–22. Print.

Hood explains how she uses miscue analysis, interviews, and observations of her students to get to know them as readers. Among other things, she observes children to understand their knowledge about texts and their textual preferences, and she pays attention to young children's independent book-handling knowledge. Hood examines patterns of miscues and strategies used by three different children and describes how she uses these data to guide her instruction.

Johnston, Peter H.
Choice Words: How Our Language Affects Children's Learning.
Portland, ME: Stenhouse, 2004. Print

Johnston helps teachers understand that the words teachers choose to use during instruction can keep the learning relationship productive and growing. This book helps educators remember that there is an important emotional side to learning. Johnston provides prompts in each chapter to help teachers think about how to use language to name what children know and to build an identity of "one who knows" in each and every child.

Peterson, Ralph.
Life in a Crowded Place: Making a Learning Community.
Portsmouth, NH: Heinemann, 1992. Print.

This book reveals the importance of creating environments in which learners value one another, live in story worlds together, and become one through social and revealing literary experiences. It reminds us what it feels like to be a young learner among many other diverse learners. Peterson provides detailed descriptions of how to create classrooms in which all children are supported and valued and where they achieve well beyond what they might have without such support.

Peterson, Ralph, and Maryann Eeds.
Grand Conversations: Literature Groups in Action.
New York: Scholastic, 1990. Print.

Ralph Peterson and Maryann Eeds explore the power of creating classrooms in which children have real conversations about real literature, broadening the definition of *reading* to encompass the stimulating, energizing practice of deep thought as it pertains to the written word. Peterson and Eeds illustrate the transformative nature of forming, sharing, and honoring multiple perspectives on quality pieces of literature.

Ray, Katie Wood.
Wondrous Words: Writers and Writing in the Elementary Classroom.
Urbana, IL: NCTE, 1999. Print.

Wondrous Words challenges teachers to know writing and to improve their craft by paying close attention to process and product. Katie Wood Ray gives specific techniques for teaching structure, word choice, and other author crafts and recommends picture books that help provide demonstrations for instruction. This text is theoretically sound and eminently practical.

Routman, Regie.
Reading Essentials: The Specifics You Need to Teach Reading Well.
Portsmouth, NH: Heinemann, 2003. Print.

Routman offers educators teaching and practice tips as well as demonstrations on how to make the teaching of reading a more thoughtful and meaningful process for readers. The book includes lesson plans, ideas, and strategies to help readers enjoy and understand text. Routman's ideas are consistent with learning theory and research and reflect her love of reading with students.

Stephens, Diane, ed.
What Matters? A Primer for Teaching Reading.
Portsmouth, NH: Heinemann, 1990. Print.

Stephens has found that teachers want to know how theory translates into practice in the classroom. Relying on her more than twenty years of teaching students, conducting research, and working with teachers, she helps us understand that teachers can help students become lifelong readers by knowing about language, learners, and teaching.

Learning about Teaching Preschool Readers
(Hope Reardon)

Clay, Marie M.
What Did I Write? Beginning Writing Behaviour.
Portsmouth, NH: Heinemann, 1975. Print.

Clay highlights and closely examines the different stages of a young child as he or she learns to write. She gives specific examples of children's writing as they move through these stages and explains what the child is attempting to achieve. Toward the end of the book, Clay makes explicit the connections between reading and writing in young children.

Owocki, Gretchen.
Literacy through Play.
Portsmouth, NH: Heinemann, 1999. Print.

In this classic resource, Owocki explains the importance of play in a young child's learning, taking the reader into two different classrooms to explain how children use play to learn about the world around them. This book is full of wonderful examples for teachers to try out in their own classrooms.

Owocki, Gretchen.
Literate Days: Reading and Writing with Preschool and Primary Children.
Portsmouth, NH: Heinemann, 2007. Print.

This is an outstanding three-book set that looks at reading and writing with preschool and primary-age children. The first book sets the stage for procedures and routines, the second helps build a literacy curriculum, and the third looks at class-room community. This set contains thirty-three lessons, a teacher's guide, and a DVD of class-room footage that shows Literate Days in action.

Pinnell, Gay Su, and Irene C. Fountas.
Literacy Beginnings: A Prekindergarten Handbook.
Portsmouth, NH: Heinemann, 2011. Print.

This recent book from Pinnell and Fountas looks specifically at the literacy growth of preschool children. It features seven large sections covering the classroom environment, language, supporting emergent readers and writers, assessment, learning about letters, sounds and words, and Fountas and Pinnell's continuum of learning. The appendixes are full of ideas for teachers to adapt to their own classrooms.

Learning about Teaching Kindergarten and First-Grade Readers (Pamela C. Jewett, Tasha Tropp Laman, Ryan Brunson, Louise Ward, and Kristy C. Wood)

Ditzel, Resi J.
Great Beginnings: Creating a Literacy-Rich Kindergarten.
York, ME: Stenhouse, 2000. Print.

Great Beginnings is a guide to teaching full-day kindergarten, providing step-by-step suggestions for a kindergarten curriculum, with a special emphasis on literacy. Putting students at the center of her classroom, the author describes how she supports her students as independent thinkers,

strategic readers, confident writers, and excited learners.

Fisher, Bobbi, and Emily Fisher Medvic.
Perspectives on Shared Reading: Planning and Practice.
Portsmouth, NH: Heinemann, 2000. Print.

Always placing students firmly at the center of the classroom and viewing learning as a natural event, Fisher and Medvic zero in on shared reading. Drawing on twenty-five years of teaching, Fisher discusses the relationship between bedtime stories and classroom reading and the theories that underlie shared reading. Medvic brings her perspective as a beginning teacher to the topic, detailing her approaches to shared reading as well as the strategies she uses with a variety of shared reading texts.

Horn, Martha, and Mary Ellen Giacobbe.
Talking, Drawing, Writing: Lessons for Our Youngest Writers.
Portland, ME: Stenhouse, 2007. Print.

This book is about the roles of talking and drawing as young children learn to write. In the introduction, the authors explain that their book is about looking and listening and "teaching young children the craft of writing by beginning with what they know." Organized by topic, the lessons include storytelling, drawing, writing, assessing, moving students forward in their writing, and more. This text is not intended as a writing manual; rather, it was written to give teachers a sense of what is possible when young children talk, draw, and write.

Miller, Debbie.
Reading with Meaning: Teaching Comprehension in the Primary Grades.
Portland, ME: Stenhouse, 2002. Print.

Miller defines and describes the thinking process-es a young child uses to understand and explores what a first-grade teacher can do to facilitate those processes. She takes us through the course of a year as she teaches comprehension strategies. Along the way, she reveals the processes she uses to immerse children in a rigorous and engaging learning environment and follows this description with an explanation of the methods she uses for introducing and developing a range of comprehension strategies.

Ray, Katie Wood, and Matt Glover.
Already Ready: Nurturing Writers in Preschool and Kindergarten.
Portsmouth, NH: Heinemann, 2008. Print.

Ray and Glover write that what brought them together was their "mutual fascination with the intellectual lives of preschoolers," and this book details the complex and sophisticated thinking that young children use when they write. In the first section of the book, readers learn what it means to be a young writer and about the importance of making picture books, rethinking the meaning of writing development, and developing children's image of self as writer. The second section focuses on how teachers can understand, support, and nurture young writers with a repertoire of classroom practices. The authors explain that they wrote this book so that teachers could notice, name, and appreciate the intricate thinking processes in which young children engage as they write.

Learning about Teaching Second- and Third-Grade Readers
(Robin W. Cox, Heidi Mills, Sandy Pirkle Anfin, and Timothy O'Keefe)

Edelsky, Carole, Karen Smith, and Christian Faltis.
Side-by-Side Learning: Exemplary Literacy Practices for English Language Learners and English Speakers in the Mainstream Classroom.
New York: Scholastic, 2008. Print.

This book and companion DVD feature critical insights and instructional strategies that unite literacy learning and inquiry for both English language learners and native English speakers. The authors feature elementary teachers who have successfully engaged diverse learners in inquiry-based curricula. The companion DVD shows teachers and students at work, and the book provides rich examples of planning templates, artifacts of student learning, and clear descriptions of strategies for scaffolding diverse literacy learners into and through inquiry. The featured teachers help readers remember the value of talking, reading, and writing to learn and the importance of curricula that are grounded in students' interests, questions, strengths, and needs.

Harvey, Stephanie, and Anne Goudvis.
Strategies That Work: Teaching Comprehension for Understanding and Engagement.
2nd ed.
Portland, ME: Stenhouse, 2007. Print.

This highly acclaimed book is useful in helping teachers think about what it means to comprehend and how to help students engage in meaningful conversations around texts. In the expanded text of the second edition, the authors address the issues of assessment, teaching students to monitor for comprehension, and how to launch lessons on comprehension.

Miller, Donalyn.
The Book Whisperer: Awakening the Inner Reader in Every Child.
San Francisco: Jossey-Bass, 2009. Print.

This book is not devoted exclusively to teaching second- and third-grade readers. In fact, Miller is a sixth-grade teacher. This is one of those theoretically sound and practically relevant gems with the potential to have a profound impact on independent reading practices across grade levels. This brilliant teacher-author makes a compelling case for independent reading and provides practical illustrations of what a truly effective reading program looks like. The advice offered can be easily and effectively transferred and transformed to support independent reading programs across grade levels and student populations.

Mills, Heidi, Timothy O'Keefe, and Louise B. Jennings.
> *Looking Closely and Listening Carefully: Learning Literacy through Inquiry.*
> Urbana, IL: NCTE, 2004. Print.

Second- and third-grade teacher Tim O'Keefe demonstrates how he teaches readers and writers through inquiry. Readers are walked through a typical day in Tim's classroom by vicariously experiencing the curricular structures and instructional strategies that make a difference: exploration, morning meeting, reading and writing workshops, daily read-alouds, math workshop, and integrated units of study in the sciences and social sciences. Tim's instructional decisions are grounded in his careful kidwatching, and one chapter is devoted to a thorough and thoughtful analysis of the relationship between his kidwatching observations and his teaching moves and their impact on two diverse literacy learners. Tim is the kind of classroom teacher who illustrates what is possible when teachers and students engage in rigorous, meaning-centered, inquiry-based literacy experiences.

Szymusiak, Karen, Franki Sibberson, and Lisa Koch.
> *Beyond Leveled Books: Supporting Early and Transitional Readers in Grades K–5.* **2nd ed.**
> Portland, ME: Stenhouse, 2008. Print.

This practical and engaging resource is appreciated by teachers of early and transitional readers across schools and districts. In the second edition, the authors and contributors provide resources to help teachers understand and teach the transitional readers in their classrooms. They address the use of independent reading and provide lists of texts to support readers.

Learning about Teaching Fourth- and Fifth-Grade Readers
(Amy Donnelly, Erika R. Cartledge, and Amy Oswalt)

Anderson, Jeff.
> *Mechanically Inclined: Building Grammar, Usage, and Style into Writer's Workshop.*
> Portland, ME: Stenhouse, 2005. Print.

Anderson reminds teachers that "[k]ids have reasons for doing what they do, even if it is flawed." Grounded in that understanding, this text helps teachers refine their understandings of grammar and mechanics. Using the thirty-five lessons in Part II of the book, teachers can help children understand and do "the things readers expect a courteous writer to do." Many teachers do not consider themselves experts in grammar; this book will inspire them to learn about grammar and to help children develop an excited and inquiring attitude about how grammar and punctuation work in a text.

Bear, Donald R., Marcia Invernizzi, Shane Templeton, and Francine Johnston.
> *Words Their Way: Word Study for Phonics, Vocabulary, and Spelling Instruction.* **3rd ed.**
> Upper Saddle River, NJ: Pearson, 2004. Print.

Teachers will use several quick reference elements of this book again and again. One is the developmental spelling stages and corresponding word study activities found inside the front and back covers. Two other incredibly useful quick references are the glossary of definitions and an appendix with word sorts organized by spelling stages. Also, the English language learning teaching notes found throughout the chapters will help teachers think through how they might adapt instruction to learn from and with their ELL learners.

Fountas, Irene C., and Gay Su Pinnell.
Guiding Readers and Writers, Grades 3-6:
Teaching Comprehension, Genre, and
Content Literacy.
Portsmouth, NH: Heinemann, 2001. Print.

The authors argue that "[e]ffective teaching in the intermediate grades begins with what we know about learners and their literacy journey," and they detail how reading and writing workshop can be utilized by upper-elementary teachers. This is a terrific, jam-packed, comprehensive resource that provides examples of mini-lessons, templates for graphic organizers, lists of leveled books, and photographs of classrooms. Section topics include independent reading, literature study, guided reading, teaching for comprehension, and the reading and writing connection, and within each section are suggestions for working with struggling readers and writers. This book is a resource that teachers in grades 3–6 should not be without. They will appreciate in particular the mini-lessons, especially "Independent Reading: The First Twenty Days of Teaching" in Chapter 9.

Sibberson, Franki, and Karen Szymusiak.
Still Learning to Read: Teaching Students in
Grades 3-6.
Portland, ME: Stenhouse, 2003. Print.

The fact that most children in fifth grade "read" influences the quality of reading instruction, however unintentionally. Sibberson and Szymusiak's book reminds teachers that if we want children to continually grow as readers, we must believe that all of us are "still learning to read." The text boxes, photographs, and children's samples throughout the book offer practical and real examples and references when planning reading instruction. Teachers will find themselves using the wide sidebar in this text to record their thinking. Chapter 5, "Grouping Beyond Levels," will help teachers make better use of anecdotal notes to make instruction more effective for every reader.

References

Abrahamson, D. (1984). To Beth's first-grade teacher. *Houston Chronicle*, p. 15.

Allington, R. L., & Johnston, P. H. (2000). *What do we know about effective fourth-grade teachers and their classrooms?* (CELA Research Report No. 13010). Albany, NY: National Research Center on English Learning and Achievement.

Allington, R. L., & Johnston, P. H. (2001). What do we know about effective fourth-grade teachers and their classrooms? In C. Roller (Ed.), *Learning to teach reading: Setting the research agenda* (pp. 150–165). Newark, DE: International Reading Association.

Anderson, C. (2000). *How's it going? A practical guide to conferring with student writers.* Portsmouth, NH: Heinemann.

Anderson, R. C., Hiebert, E. H., Scott, J. A., & Wilkinson, I. A. G. (1985). *Becoming a nation of readers: The report of the Commission on Reading.* Washington, DC: The National Institute of Education.

Anthony, R. J., Johnson, T. D., Mickelson, N. I., & Preece, A. (1991). *Evaluating literacy: A perspective for change.* Portsmouth, NH: Heinemann.

Batsche, G. M., Curtis, M. J., Dorman, C., Castillo, J. M., & Porter, L. J. (2007). The Florida problem-solving/response to intervention model: Implementing a statewide initiative. In S. R. Jimerson, M. K. Burns, & A. M. VanDerHeyden (Eds.), *Handbook of response to intervention: The science and practice of assessment and intervention* (pp. 378–395). New York: Springer.

Beechen, A. (2003). *Holly jolly Jimmy: The Adventures of Jimmy Neutron, boy genius.* New York: Simon Spotlight/Nickelodeon.

Blachman, B. A., Schatschneider, C., Fletcher, J. M., & Clonan, S. M. (2003). Early reading intervention: A classroom prevention study and a remediation study. In B. R. Foorman (Ed.), *Preventing and remediating reading difficulties: Bringing science to scale* (pp. 253–271). Baltimore: York Press.

Bomer, R. (2007). When writing leads: An activity-theoretic account of the literate activity of first graders stronger at writing than reading. In D. W. Rowe, R. T. Jiménez, D. L. Compton, D. K. Dickinson, Y. Kim, K. M. Leander, & V. J. Risko (Eds.), *56th yearbook of the National Reading Conference* (pp. 151-163). Oak Creek, WI: National Reading Conference.

Bond, G. L., & Dykstra, R. (1967). The cooperative research program in first-grade reading instruction. *Reading Research Quarterly, 2*(4), 5–142. Reprinted in *Reading Research Quarterly*, 1997, *32*(4), 345–427.

Bridwell, N. (1963). *Clifford the big red dog.* New York: Cartwheel Books.

Buffett, J. (2008). *Swine not? A novel pig tale.* New York: Little, Brown and Company.

Calkins, L., Montgomery, K. & Santman, D. (1998). *A teacher's guide to standardized reading tests: Knowledge is power.* Portsmouth, NH: Heinemann.

Cambourne, B. (1987). Language, learning and literacy. In A. Butler & J. Turbill, *Towards a reading-writing classroom* (pp. 5–10). Portsmouth, NH: Heinemann.

Cambourne, B. (1995). Toward an educationally relevant theory of literacy learning: Twenty years of inquiry. *The Reading Teacher, 49*(3), 182–190.

Carle, E. (2004). *Mister Seahorse.* New York: Philomel Books.

Chomsky, C. (1971). Write first, read later. *Childhood Education, 47*(6), 296–299.

Clay, M. M. (1993). *An observation survey of early literacy achievement.* Portsmouth, NH: Heinemann.

Clay, M. M. (1998). *By different paths to common outcomes.* York, ME: Stenhouse.

Cox, R. W. (2012). *Beyond "best practices": An examination of teachers, teaching, and reading achievement* (Unpublished doctoral dissertation). University of South Carolina, Columbia.

Crismore, A. (Ed.). (1985). *Landscapes: A state-of-the-art assessment of reading comprehension research, 1974–1984.* Bloomington, IN: Language Education Department.

Darling-Hammond, L. (2000). Teacher quality and student achievement: A review of state policy evidence. *Education Policy Analysis Archives, 8*(1), 1–44. Retrieved from http://epaa.asu.edu/ojs/article/view/392

Data Recognition Corporation. (2009). Palmetto Assessment of State Standards (PASS). Retrieved from https://sc.drcedirect.com

Davenport, M. R. (2002). *Miscues not mistakes: Reading assessment in the classroom.* Portsmouth, NH: Heinemann.

DeFord, D. E. (2004). *Dominie reading and writing assessment portfolio.* Carlsbad, CA: Dominie Press. Now retrievable online at http://www.pearsonschool.com/index.cfm?locator=PSZu68&PMDbProgramId=19381

Denton, C. A., Vaughn, S., & Fletcher, J. M. (2003). Bringing research-based practice in reading intervention to scale. *Learning Disabilities: Research and Practice, 18*(3), 201–211.

Duffy, G. G. (1983). From turn taking to sense making: Broadening the concept of reading teacher effectiveness. *Journal of Educational Research, 76*(3), 134–139.

Duffy, G. G., Roehler, L. R., & Putnam, J. (1987). Putting the teacher in control: Basal reading textbooks and instructional decision making. *The Elementary School Journal, 87*(3), 357–366.

Eastman, P. D. (1961). *Go dog go!* New York: Random House.

Edwards, N. (2009). *Dog whisperer: The rescue.* New York: Square Fish.

Eitelgeorge, J. S., Wilson, G. P., & Kent, K. (2007). Using informal assessments to monitor and support literacy progress. In P. Jones, J. F. Carr, & R. L. Ataya (Eds.), *A pig don't get fatter the more you weigh it: Classroom assessments that work* (pp. 51–68). New York: Teachers College Press.

Elbow, P. (2004). Write first: Putting writing before reading is an effective approach to teaching and learning. *Educational Leadership, 62*(2), 8–14.

Ferguson, R. F. (1991). Paying for public education: New evidence on how and why money matters. *Harvard Journal on Legislation, 28*(2), 465–498.

Ferreiro, E., & Teberosky, A. (1982). *Literacy before schooling.* Portsmouth, NH: Heinemann.

Fox, M. (2002). *Sleepy bears.* New York: Houghton Mifflin.

Frost, E. (1991). *Case of the missing chick* (Big book ed.). New York: Troll.

Galdone, P. (2008). *The three billy goats gruff.* New York: Clarion Books.

Genishi, C., & Haas Dyson, A. (2009). *Children, language, and literacy: Diverse learners in diverse times.* New York: Teacher College Press.

Giff, P. R. (1990). *Ronald Morgan goes to bat.* New York: Puffin Books.

Goodman, Y. M. (1978). Kid watching: An alternative to testing. *National Elementary Principal, 57*(4), 41–45.

Goodman, Y. M., and Burke, C. L. (1972). *Reading miscue inventory manual: Procedure for diagnosis and evaluation.* New York: Macmillan.

Goodman, Y. M., Watson, D. J., & Burke, C. L. (1987). *Reading miscue inventory: Alternative procedures.* New York: Owen.

Halliday, M. A. K. (1969). Relevant models of language. *Educational Review, 22*(1), 26–37.

Halliday, M. A. K. (1973). *Explorations in the Functions of Language.* London: Edward Arnold.

Halliday, M. A. K. (1975). *Learning how to mean: Explorations in the development of language.* London: Edward Arnold.

Halliday, M. A. K. (1980). Three Aspects of Children's Language Development: Learning Language, Learning through Language, Learning about Language. In Y. M. Goodman, M. M. Haussler, & D. S. Strickland (Eds.), *Oral and written language development: Impact on schools. Proceedings from the 1979 and 1980 IMPACT conferences* (pp. 7–19). Newark, DE: International Reading Association; Urbana, IL: National Council of Teachers of English.

Hanushek, E. A., Kain, J. F., & Rivkin, S. G. (2002). Inferring program effects for special populations: Does special education raise academic achievement for students with disabilities? *Review of Economics and Statistics, 84*(4), 584–599.

Harste, J. C., Woodward, V. A., & Burke, C. L. (1984). *Language stories and literacy lessons.* Portsmouth, NH: Heinemann.

Harvey, S., & Goudvis, A. (2007). *Strategies that*

work: Teaching comprehension for understanding and engagement (2nd ed.). York, ME: Stenhouse.

Hesse, K. (1996). *The music of dolphins*. New York: Scholastic Press.

Hindley, J. (1996). *In the company of children*.York, ME: Stenhouse.

Hohmann, M., Weikart, D. P., & Epstein, A. S. (2008). *Educating young children: Active learning practices for preschool and child care programs* (3rd ed.). Ypsilanti, MI: High/Scope Press.

Hubbard, R. S., & Power, B. M. (1993). *The art of classroom inquiry: A handbook for teacher-researchers*. Portsmouth, NH: Heinemann.

Individuals with Disabilities Education Improvement Act of 2004, Pub. L. No. 108-446, 118 Stat. 2647 (2004). Retrieved from http://idea.ed.gov/download/statute.html

International Reading Association, and National Council of Teachers of English. (1996). *Standards for the English language arts*. Newark, DE: IRA; Urbana, IL: NCTE.

IRA–NCTE Joint Task Force on Assessment. (2010). *Standards for the assessment of reading and writing* (Rev. ed.). Newark, DE: International Reading Association; Urbana, IL: National Council of Teachers of English.

James, W. (1890). *The principles of psychology* (Vol. 1). New York: Holt.

Johnson, P. (2006). *One child at a time: Making the most of your time with struggling readers, K–6*. Portland, ME: Stenhouse.

Johnston, P. (1997). *Knowing literacy: Constructive literacy assessment*. Portland, ME: Stenhouse.

Johnston, P. (2004). *Choice words: How our language affects children's learning*. Portland, ME: Stenhouse.

Johnston, P. (2005). Literacy assessment and the future. *The Reading Teacher, 58*(7), 684–686.

Kavale, K. A., & Reese, J. H. (1991). Teacher beliefs and perceptions about learning disabilities: A survey of Iowa practitioners. *Learning Disability Quarterly, 14*(2), 141–160.

Kindersley, D. (1990). *Amazing birds* (Eyewitness Juniors series). New York: Knopf Books for Young Readers.

Ladson-Billings, G. (1994). *The dreamkeepers: Successful teachers of African-American children*. San Francisco: Jossey-Bass.

Langer, J. A. (2000). Excellence in English in middle and high school: How teachers' professional lives support student achievement. *American Educational Research Journal, 37*(2), 397–439.

Littlesugar, A. (2001). *Freedom school, yes!* New York: Philomel Books.

Lobel, A. (1972). *Frog and toad together*. New York: Harper Collins.

MacLachlan, P. (1994). *Skylark*. New York: Harper Collins.

MacLachlan, P. (2001). *Caleb's story*. New York: Joanna Cotler Books.

Mardell-Czudnowski, C., & Goldenberg, D. S. (1998). *DIAL-3: Developmental indicators for the assessment of learning* (3rd ed.). Circle Pines, MN: American Guidance Service.

McDonald, M. (2000). *Judy Moody*, Cambridge, MA: Candlewick Press.

McGill-Franzen, A., Allington, R. L., Yokoi, L., & Brooks, G. (1999). Putting books in the classroom seems necessary but not sufficient. *The Journal of Educational Research, 93*(2), 67–74.

Mills, H. (Guest Ed.). (2005). Broadening visions of what counts: Assessment as knowing and being known [Special Issue]. *School Talk, 11*(1), 7.

Mills, (with O'Keefe, T.). (2011). Inquiry into assessment strategies: From kidwatching to responsive teaching. *Talking Points, 22*(2), 2–8.

Mills, H., O'Keefe, T., & Jennings, L. B. (2004). *Looking closely and listening carefully: Learning literacy through inquiry*. Urbana, IL: National Council of Teachers of English.

Morrow, L. M. (with Wamsley, G., Duhammel, K., & Fittipaldi, N.). (2002). A case study of exemplary practice in fourth grade. In B. M. Taylor & P. D. Pearson (Eds.), *Teaching reading: Effective schools, accomplished teachers* (pp. 289–307). Mahwah, NJ: Erlbaum.

Munson, D. (2000). *Enemy pie*. San Francisco: Chronicle Books.

Murphy, S. J. (2003). *Double the ducks*. New York: Harper Collins.

Muth, J. J. (2002). *The three questions*. New York: Scholastic Press.

National Center for Education Statistics. (1994). *Data compendium for the NAEP 1992 reading assess-*

ment of the nation and the states: 1992 NAEP trial state assessment. Washington, DC: U.S. Department of Education.

Nelson, J. M., & Machek, G. R. (2007). A survey of training, practice, and competence in reading assessment and intervention. *School Psychology Review, 36*(2), 311–327.

Nieto, S. (1999). *The light in their eyes: Creating multicultural learning communities.* New York: Teachers College Press.

Northwest Evaluation Association. (2008). *MAP® for Primary Grades* [computerized assessment system]. Portland, OR: Author.

Omalza, S., Aihara, K., & Stephens, D. (1997). Engaged in learning through the HT process. *Primary Voices K–6, 5*(1), 4–17.

Osborne, M. P. (1992). *Dinosaurs before dark* (Magic Tree House series). New York: Random House Books for Young Readers.

Osborne, M. P. (2000a). *Civil War on Sunday* (Magic Tree House series). New York: Random House Books for Young Readers.

Osborne, M. P. (2000b). *Revolutionary War on Wednesday* (Magic Tree House series). New York: Random House Books for Young Readers.

Owocki, G., & Goodman, Y. (2002). *Kidwatching: Documenting children's literacy development.* Portsmouth, NH: Heinemann.

Paley, V. G. (1981). *Wally's stories: Conversations in the kindergarten.* Cambridge, MA: Harvard University Press.

Paley, V. G. (1990). *The boy who would be a helicopter: The uses of storytelling in the classroom.* Cambridge, MA: Harvard University Press.

Pearson, P. D., & Fielding, L. (1991). Comprehension instruction. In R. Barr, M. L. Kamil, P. Mosenthal, & P. D. Pearson (Eds.), *Handbook of reading research* (Vol. 2, pp. 815–860). New York: Longman.

Pearson, P. D., & Gallagher, M. C. (1983). The instruction of reading comprehension. *Contemporary Educational Psychology, 8*(3), 317–344.

Peterson, R., & Eads, M. (1990). *Grand conversations: Literature groups in action.* New York: Scholastic.

Polacco, P. (1998). *Thank you, Mr. Falker.* New York: Philomel Books.

Pressley, M., Rankin, J., & Yokoi, L. (1996). A survey of instructional practices of primary teachers nominated as effective in promoting literacy. *The Elementary School Journal, 96*(4), 363–384.

Raffi. (1987). *Down by the bay (Raffi songs to read).* New York: Crown Books.

Rappaport, D. (2001). *Martin's big words: The life of Martin Luther King, Jr.* New York: Hyperion Books for Children.

Rasinski, T. V., Padak, N. D., & Fawcett, G. (2010). *Teaching children who find reading difficult* (4th ed.). Boston: Allyn and Bacon.

Rawls, W. (1961). *Where the red fern grows: The story of two dogs and a boy.* Garden City, NY: Doubleday.

Riordan, R. (2005). *The lightening thief.* New York: Hyperion Books.

Riordan, R. (2010). *The lost hero* (The Heroes of Olympus series).New York: Disney-Hyperion Books.

Routman, R. (1996). *Literacy at the crossroads: Crucial talk about reading, writing, and other teaching dilemmas.* Portsmouth, NH: Heinemann.

Sachar, L. (1998). *Holes.* New York: Farrar, Straus and Giroux.

Sanders, W. L. (1998, December). Value-added assessment: A method for measuring the effects of the system, school and teacher on the rate of student academic success. *The School Administrator 55*(11). Retrieved from http://www.aasa.org/SchoolAdministratorArticle.aspx?id=15066

Scanlon, D. M., & Anderson, K. L. (2010). Using the interactive strategies approach to prevent reading difficulties in an RTI context. In M. Y. Lipson & K. K. Wixson (Eds.), *Successful approaches to RTI: Collaborative practices for improving K–12 Literacy* (pp. 20–65). Newark, DE: International Reading Association.

Scanlon, D. M., Vellutino, F. R., Small, S. G., Fanuele, D. P., & Sweeney, J. M. (2005). Severe reading difficulties—can they be prevented? A comparison of prevention and intervention approaches. *Exceptionality: A Special Education Journal, 13*(4), 209–227.

Short, K. G., Harste, J. C., & Burke, C. (1996). *Creating classrooms for authors and inquirers* (2nd ed.). Portsmouth, NH: Heinemann. Sibberson, F., & Szymusiak, K. (2003). *Still learning to read: Teaching students in grades 3–6.* Portland, ME: Stenhouse.

Sipay, E. R. (1968). Interpreting the USOE cooperative reading studies. *The Reading Teacher, 22*(1), 10–16, 35.

Smith, C. A., & Downing, N. L. (1993). *The peaceful classroom: 162 easy activities to teach preschoolers compassion and cooperation.* Mt. Rainier, MD: Gryphon House.

Smith, F. (1978). *Understanding reading: A psycholinguistic analysis of reading and learning to read* (2nd ed.). New York: Holt, Rinehart and Winston.

Smith, F. (1987). *Joining the literacy club: Further essays into education.* Portsmouth, NH: Heinemann.

Smith, F. (1992). Learning to read: The never-ending debate. *Phi Delta Kappan 73*(6), 432–35, 438–41.

Stephens, D. (Ed.). (1990). *What matters? A primer for teaching reading.* Portsmouth, NH: Heinemann.

Stephens, D. (2005). *Skinny strips.* Unpublished instructional tool.

Stephens, D., & Story, J. (Eds.). (2000). *Assessment as inquiry: Learning the hypothesis–test process.* Urbana, IL: National Council of Teachers of English.

Stephens, D., et al. (1996). When assessment is inquiry. *Language Arts, 73*(2), 105–112.

Strickland, K., & Strickland, J. (2000). *Making assessment elementary.* Portsmouth, NH: Heinemann.

Taberski, S. (2000). *On solid ground: Strategies for teaching reading K–3.* Portsmouth, NH: Heinemann.

Taylor, B. M. (2002). Highly accomplished primary grade teachers in effective schools. In B. M. Taylor & P. D. Pearson (Eds.), *Teaching reading: Effective schools and accomplished teachers* (pp. 279–287). Mahwah, NJ: Erlbaum.

Taylor, B. M., Pearson, P. D., Clark, K., & Walpole, S. (2000). Effective schools and accomplished teachers: Lessons about primary-grade reading instruction in low-income schools. *Elementary School Journal, 101*(2), 121–165.

Taylor, B. M., Pearson, P. D., Peterson, D. S., & Rodriguez, M. C. (2003). Reading growth in high-poverty classrooms: The influence of teacher practices that encourage cognitive engagement in literacy learning. *Elementary School Journal, 104*(1), 3–28.

Teague, M. (1994). *Pigsty.* New York: Scholastic.

Torgesen, J. K., Alexander, A. W., Wagner, R. K., Rashotte, C. A., Voeller, K. K. S., & Conway, T. (2001). Intensive remedial instruction for children with severe reading disabilities: Immediate and long-term outcomes from two instructional approaches. *Journal of Learning Disabilities, 34*(1), 33–58, 78.

Torgesen, J. K., Rashotte, C., Alexander, A., Alexander, J., & MacPhee, K. (2003). Progress toward understanding the instructional conditions necessary for remediating reading difficulties in older children. In B. R. Foorman (Ed.), *Preventing and remediating reading difficulties: Bringing science to scale* (pp. 275–298). Baltimore, MD: York Press.

Vellutino, F. R., Scanlon, D. M., & Tanzman, M. S. (1998). The case for early intervention in diagnosing specific reading disability. *Journal of School Psychology, 36*(4), 367–397.

Visovatti, K. (1994). Developing primary voices. *Primary Voices K–6, 2*(2), 8–19.

Vygotsky, L. S. (1978). *Mind in society: The development of higher psychological processes.* Cambridge, MA: Harvard University Press.

Watson, D. (1992). What exactly do you mean by the term "kidwatching"? In O. Cochrane (Ed.), *Questions and answers about whole language* (pp. 98–104). Katonah, NY: Owen.

Wharton-McDonald, R., Pressley, M., & Hampston, J. M. (1998). Literacy instruction in nine first-grade classrooms: Teacher characteristics and student achievement. *Elementary School Journal, 99*(2), 101–128.

White, E. B. (2004). *Charlotte's web.* New York: Harper Collins. (Original work published 1952)

Whitin, D. J., Mills H., & O'Keefe, T. (1991). *Living and learning mathematics: Stories and strategies for supporting mathematical learning.* Portsmouth, NH: Heinemann.

Willems, M. (2003). *Don't let the pigeon drive the bus!* New York: Hyperion Books.

Williams, L. (1986). *The little old lady who was not afraid of anything.* New York: Harper Collins.

Wixson, K. K., Lipson, M. Y., & Johnston, P. H. (2010). Making the most of RTI. In M. Y. Lipson & K. K. Wixson (Eds.), *Successful approaches to RTI: Collaborative practices for improving K–12 literacy* (pp. 1–19). Newark, DE: International Reading Association.

Wolcott, H. F. (2009). *Writing up qualitative research* (3rd ed.). Thousand Oaks, CA: Sage.

Wood, A. (1984). *The napping house*. New York: Harcourt.

Ysseldyke, J. E., Thurlow, M. L., Mecklenburg, C., & Graden, J. (1984). Opportunity to learn for regular and special education students during reading instruction. *Remedial and Special Education, 5*(1), 29–37.

Index

Editor

Diane Stephens is the Swearingen Chair of Education at the University of South Carolina. She received her doctorate from Indiana University and began her career working with high school dropouts. She has subsequently worked with readers from ages six to sixty, focusing on elementary school children not considered to be reading at grade level. She has conducted research on assessment and decision making, teachers as learners, and the impact of large-scale professional development efforts. Stephens led the smaller scale, three-year-long professional development effort with which the authors of the case studies in this book were involved. She and those teachers have presented nationally and published an October 2012 *Reading Teacher* article on their work. This is her second edited book with NCTE; the first, with Jennifer Story, was *Assessment as Inquiry: Learning the Hypothesis-Test Process* (1999).

Contributors

Sandy Pirkle Anfin has been an educator for seven years. She earned her BA in early childhood education from Clemson University and an MEd in language and literacy from the University of South Carolina. During her master's program, she worked as a graduate assistant for the Department of Language and Literacy, and she has an additional thirty hours of literacy course work as well as National Board Certification in literacy. Anfin currently teaches third grade in a diverse Title I school in South Carolina. She has presented at the South Carolina Formative Assessment Conference as well as several district professional development sessions and facilitated a professional leaning community (PLC) at her school. She is passionate about creating a classroom culture that allows all students to see themselves as readers and writers and about using data to inform instructional decisions.

Ryan Brunson is a first-grade teacher at Ben Hazel Elementary School in Hampton, South Carolina. She has been a K–1 teacher for twelve years, the first two at Varnville Elementary and the last ten at Ben Hazel. Brunson earned her bachelor's degree from the University of South Carolina in 2000. She strongly believes that her instruction needs to begin with her individual first-grade students, and she uses a variety of assessment tools to inquire about their strengths and areas in which they need support.

Erika R. Cartledge, a National Board Certified Teacher, has been an educator for more than twenty years and believes that teaching is her divine calling. She earned her BS in elementary education from Winthrop University and an MEd in elementary education and an EdS in language and literacy from the University of South Carolina. She currently teaches fourth grade in a South Carolina public school. Cartledge's experiences include serving as a literacy coach and mentor, providing professional development, and leading study groups and professional book clubs. She continues to be a teacher-learner and a keen kidwatcher.

Robin W. Cox is an instructional specialist for English language arts in School District 5 of Lexington and Richland Counties in South Carolina. Prior to this position, she was a literacy coach through the South Carolina Reading Initiative in collaboration with NCTE and also taught elementary school for several years. Her passion is in working with teachers in all grades to help readers and writers be a part of the literacy club. Cox has worked closely with Diane Stephens to develop an RTI model for reaching children in need of intervention services. As a part of that work, Robin coauthored a *Reading Teacher* article on the work in her district.

Diane E. DeFord is the Swearingen Literacy Chair at the University of South Carolina. She teaches courses on reading and writing methods and assessment and instructional decision making at the undergraduate and master's levels, as well as a variety of doctorate-level courses. She is the author of *Dominie Reading and Writing Assessment Portfolio*, and she has written many book chapters, journal articles, and books for young children. DeFord remains active in Reading Recovery as a trainer emeritus and does professional development for teachers on such topics as literacy coaching, assessment, teaching through children's strengths in support of new learning, and tutoring emergent readers and writers.

Amy Donnelly is an associate professor of elementary education and language and literacy at the University of South Carolina, and she was the founding principal and research specialist at the Center for Inquiry, initially a university–public school of choice. She has devoted her career to working collaboratively with inservice and preservice teachers to expand their vision of literacy, inquiry-based instruction, and literacy assessment. Donnelly's recent work involves helping teachers better understand how to use data to grow reading proficiency and how to use standards to craft quality literacy instruction in elementary classrooms, as well as the role that language plays in helping teachers create transformative literacy practices. Other publications include *From the Ground Up: Creating a Culture of Inquiry* (2001).

Anne Downs is currently a reading interventionist at River Springs Elementary School in Irmo, South Carolina. She previously served as a literacy coach, regular classroom teacher, and teacher for the academically gifted; participated in the South Carolina Reading Initiative; and facilitated literacy learning cohorts. Most recently, Downs has concentrated on building children's reading processes and, through work with Diane Stephens, has developed systematic ways to help children develop a generative theory of reading and effective and efficient problem-solving skills and strategies. She has been an educator for more than twenty years and is Nationally Board Certified in early and middle literacy.

A graduate of the University of South Carolina, **Tammy Yvonne Spann Frierson** has been an early childhood educator for more than seventeen years. She is a gifted storyteller and uses that gift to teach and learn from the children in her multiage Montessori classroom in Elgin, South Carolina. She was awarded the Golden Apple Teaching Award, which is based on a teacher's outstanding classroom teaching methods. Frierson believes that teaching is her calling and that "God created me to do this."

Jennie Goforth is currently a reading interventionist, serving children in grades 1–5 in an elementary school near Columbia, South Carolina. She is certified in elementary education and in reading, has a master's degree in divergent learning and an education specialist degree in language and literacy, and is Nationally Board Certified in literacy. Goforth has presented at NCTE's Annual Convention and was recently part of a group that published a *Reading Teacher* article on RTI. She resides in Irmo, South Carolina, where she is married and a mother of three children.

Lisa Jaeger has a master's degree in elementary education from the University of South Carolina and has been an elementary school teacher for nine years, serving as a reading interventionist for five of those years. Most recently, she completed a three-year intensive study of reading theory and process under the guidance of Diane Stephens at the University of South Carolina. Jaeger has presented at NCTE's Whole Language Umbrella Conference and the South Carolina Literacy Conference, and was recently part of a group that published an article on RTI in *The Reading Teacher*. She lives in Lexington, South Carolina, with her husband and two children.

Pamela C. Jewett is an associate professor at the University of South Carolina, teaching courses in the MEd and PhD program in language and literacy and, as an action researcher, taking an inquiry stance toward her teaching. Her research interests center on the intersections of transactional literary theory and critical literacy theory and on children's literature written in the United States and abroad. In her most recent research, Jewett investigated how to support teachers in identifying the literacies of disciplines and incorporating them into their content area teaching.

Tasha Tropp Laman is an associate professor in the Department of Instruction and Teacher Education at the University of South Carolina, where she researches multilingual students' writing practices, the impact of school–university partnerships on preservice teachers and classroom educators over time, and the role of critical literacy in children's literacy practices. She has published her research in journals such as *Language Arts*, *The Reading Teacher*, *Equity & Excellence in Education*, *Theory Into Practice*, and *Voices in the Middle*. Laman is the author of *From Ideas to Words: Writing Strategies for English Language Learners* (2013).

Julia López-Robertson has a doctorate in language, reading, and culture from the University of Arizona and is currently an associate professor of language and literacy at the University of South Carolina. Her scholarly agenda is built on a commitment to working with children, families, teachers, and preservice teachers in public schools, universities, and communities to advance understandings about emerging bilingual/multilingual students and their families, as well as on a commitment to transform teacher education to support equitable teaching for all children, particularly English language learners. López-Robertson spent seventeen years as a bilingual primary teacher in Boston and Tucson.

Ashley Matheny is a reading interventionist, serving children in grades 2–5 in an elementary school near Columbia, South Carolina. Certified in reading and elementary education, she recently completed a three-year intensive study of reading theory and process under the guidance of Diane Stephens at the University of South Carolina. Matheny was named Teacher of the Year by her school in 2005–06 and Distinguished Reading Teacher of the Year by her district in 2009–10. She loves reading with children, reading professionally, and reading as a personal hobby.

Heidi Mills is an endowed professor in the Department of Instruction and Teacher Education at the University of South Carolina. She also serves as the curriculum, research, and development specialist at the Center for Inquiry, a magnet program and university–public school partnership in Richland School District Two. She has published six books from leading publishers in education, a professional development videotape series, and numerous articles in refereed journals featuring her collaborative research with classroom teachers. Mills's research interests include the role of inquiry in literacy and learning as well as ongoing professional development through university–school partnerships. She supports the work of classroom teachers across the state and country as a school-based consultant.

Timothy O'Keefe is a second- and third-grade teacher at the Center for Inquiry in Columbia, South Carolina. As a teacher-researcher, he has written various chapters and articles in professional journals, and his classroom has been the focus of four books and featured in several professional video series: *Scienceline*, a PBS series focusing on teaching science through inquiry; a series on teaching and reaching at-risk learners; a series on curriculum and assessment strategies; and a series funded by the Annenberg Foundation on conversations in literacy and literature. O'Keefe has consulted in schools and districts across the country on literacy, inquiry-based instruction, developing integrated curriculum and assessment strategies, and parent communication.

Amy Oswalt has a degree in elementary education from the University of South Carolina and is in her fifth year of teaching. Although she started out teaching fifth grade at Lake Murray Elementary in South Carolina, currently she teaches kindergarten at a public school in Florida.

She is passionate about using assessment to facilitate the growth of readers and writers and about including parents as partners in discovering everything children know. Oswalt believes that students learn in different ways and therefore need to demonstrate their knowledge through various means. She also believes that strong classroom communities facilitate true learning, friendship, and happiness. This makes it a pleasure for both students and teacher to come to school every day.

Kristi Plyler is a reading interventionist at a Title I elementary school and works with children in grades K–5. She recently completed a three-year study of the reading process with a group of teachers from her school district, led by Diane Stephens of the University of South Carolina. She received her MAT from the University of South Carolina in 2004 and is certified in elementary education and reading. Plyler was her school's Distinguished Reading Teacher in 2011–12. She loves to help kids learn and grow into happy, successful readers.

Hope Reardon is currently a child development teacher of four-year-olds at Hursey Elementary in Charleston, South Carolina. She has been teaching and working with young children and teachers for the past seventeen years. During her teaching career, she left the classroom for a few years to work as a South Carolina Reading First literacy coach. When the grant was finished, she went back into the classroom to work with children and her fellow teachers on best literacy practices for young children. Reardon holds a bachelor's degree from Maryville University in Saint Louis, as well as a master's degree from the University of Charleston and an education specialist degree from the University of South Carolina. She is currently working on her doctorate in language and literacy from the University of South Carolina. She loves working with all young children with emergent literacy, especially English language learners.

Lee Riser recently retired from teaching after spending the majority of her career as a special education teacher for children with developmental disabilities and learning differences. The last ten years were devoted to teaching reading to middle school and elementary students. Riser has a bachelor's degree in elementary education from Seton Hall University and an EdM in special education, as well as thirty additional hours in reading and literacy from the University of South Carolina. She lives in Chapin with her husband, John, and is the proud mother of two daughters. Lee is currently a volunteer reader with Happy Wheels, a nonprofit organization that promotes literacy and smiles with books and toys for patients at Palmetto Richland Children's Hospital.

Beth Sawyer has taught for twenty-nine years, twenty-six of those in South Carolina's public schools. For the first sixteen years of her career, Beth was a special education resource teacher in classrooms ranging from elementary to high school. In 1998 a new program established in Lexington/Richland District Five allowed her to continue working with small groups of readers. A few years later she was trained as a reading interventionist under the guidance of Diane Stephens. Sawyer currently teaches at Lake Murray Elementary School in Chapin, South Carolina. She has a bachelor's degree from Coastal Carolina University, a master's in special education from the College of Charleston, and an additional thirty hours in language and literacy from the University of South Carolina.

Lucy K. Spence is an associate professor of language and literacy at the University of South Carolina, where her research centers on linguistically diverse student writers and includes the development of a novel writing assessment, Generous Reading. This research has been published in *Language Arts*, *The Reading Teacher*, and *TESOL Journal*. She works as a literacy teacher educator and has taught onsite in eight different schools across South Carolina.

Before joining the university faculty, Spence taught grades K–8 in Arizona. She has taught in a reading program, an ESL classroom, and as a media/literacy expert in a Spanish-language-dominant community.

Tara Thompson's fifteen years of teaching include experiences in kindergarten, first grade, second grade, and reading intervention work with K–5 students. She has a reading endorsement and is National Board Certified in early childhood. She earned a master's degree in language and literacy from the University of South Carolina, where she is currently enrolled as a doctoral student. She has presented at NCTE's Annual Convention and was recently part of a group that published a *Reading Teacher* article on RTI. Thompson resides in Chapin, South Carolina. She is married and the proud mother of a ten-year-old daughter, Madison.

Kathy Vickio has been a teacher for more than fourteen years, including experience in special education, literacy coaching, and reading intervention. She is currently a reading interventionist for K–5 students at Oak Pointe Elementary School, where she was Reading Teacher of the Year in 2008. Vickio holds a bachelor's degree from the University of South Carolina and the South Carolina Honors College, as well as an MAT in special education. Her training in literacy instruction includes work with the South Carolina Reading Initiative and the Reading Intervention Cohort in School District Five of Lexington and Richland Counties under Diane Stephens. She has given several literacy presentations at conferences, in local school districts, and to parents. She is a Nationally Board Certified Teacher.

Louise Ward recently retired after thirty-eight years in the classroom. She taught kindergarten and fifth grade in parochial and public schools in New York City before moving to the Southeast, where she worked in the same school district for thirty years, teaching first grade for sixteen years, second grade for ten years, and kindergarten for four years. Ward mentored new teachers and was a coaching teacher for preservice teachers. She presented her classroom research and experiences at both local and national conferences such as NCTE and the Whole Language Umbrella's Literacies for All Summer Institute. She continues to tutor children weekly at a school near her home.

Cindy Wilcox is a reading interventionist working with grades 3–5 students in a diverse Title I elementary school. She was one of a group of ten teachers in her school district that extensively studied and collaborated in the area of language and literacy over a three-year period, led at the district level by Robin Cox and at the university level by Diane Stephens. Wilcox was her school's Reading Teacher of the Year 2011–12. She is the creator and coordinator of READ and RUN, a summer library for two apartment complexes whose children feed into her school.

Jennifer L. Wilson was an associate professor at the University of South Carolina in the Department of Instruction and Teacher Education, teaching courses in middle level literacy, including reading assessment. She was a passionate and dedicated educator who died tragically in August 2011.

Kristy C. Wood is the assistant principal of Hampton Elementary School. She has worked as an educational consultant for seven years, and before that she was an educator in Hampton District One for eleven years working as a classroom teacher in grades preK–4 and as a literacy coach. During that time, she was named Varnville Elementary Teacher of the Year, Brunson Elementary Teacher of the Year, and Hampton One District Teacher of the Year. In addition to her work with students and teachers, she has presented at numerous state and national conferences.

This book was typeset in Janson Text and BotonBQ by
Barbara Frazier.

Typefaces used on the cover include American Typewriter,
Frutiger Bold, Formata Light, and Formata Bold.

The book was printed on 60-lb. White Recycled Offset paper
by Versa Press, Inc.

30% Total Recycled Fiber